fruitfeast

fruitfeast

maggie mayhew

southwater

This edition is published by Southwater

Southwater is an imprint of
Anness Publishing Limited
Hermes House
88-89 Blackfriars Road
London SE1 8HA
tel. 020 7401 2077
fax 020 7633 9499

Distributed in the UK by
The Manning Partnership
251-253 London Road East
Batheaston
Bath BA1 7RL
tel. 01225 852 727
fax 01225 852 852

Distributed in the USA by
Anness Publishing Inc.
27 West 20th Street
Suite 504
New York NY 10011

Distributed in Australia by
Sandstone Publishing
Unit 1, 360 Norton Street
Leichhardt
New South Wales 2040
tel. 02 9560 7888
fax 02 9560 7488

All rights reserved. No part of this publication may be reproduced, stored in a retrieval system, or transmitted in any way or by any means, electronic, mechanical, photocopying, recording or otherwise, without the prior written permission of the copyright holder.

© 2001 Anness Publishing Limited

1 3 5 7 9 10 8 6 4 2

Publisher: Joanna Lorenz
Managing Editor: Linda Fraser
Editor: Susannah Blake
Designer: Nigel Partridge
Photography: William Lingwood (recipes) and Don Last (fruits)
Food for Photography: Bridget Sargeson (recipes) and Christine France (fruits)
Styling: Shannon Beare

Previously published as part of a larger compendium, *The World Encyclopedia of Fruit*

NOTES

For all recipes, quantities are given in both metric and imperial measures and, where appropriate, measures are also given in standard cups and spoons. Follow one set, but not a mixture because they are not interchangeable.

Standard spoon and cup measures are level.
1 tsp = 5ml, 1 tbsp = 15ml, 1 cup = 250ml/8fl oz

Australian standard tablespoons are 20ml. Australian readers should use 3 tsp in place of 1 tbsp for measuring small quantities of gelatine, cornflour, salt etc.

Medium eggs are used unless otherwise stated

Contents

INTRODUCTION	6
APPLE, PEAR AND QUINCE RECIPES	8
STONE FRUIT RECIPES	26
BERRY AND CURRANT RECIPES	44
CITRUS FRUIT RECIPES	66
EXOTIC FRUIT RECIPES	88
MELON, GRAPE, FIG AND RHUBARB RECIPES	114
INDEX	126

6 Introduction

Fruits are one of nature's most bountiful creations, with their vast array of colours, tastes, textures and aromas. They are not only wonderful temptations for the tastebuds, but also a supremely healthy food, bursting with health-giving nutrients and natural sugars that are so much kinder to the body than the refined sugars found in cakes and confectionery. Naturally low in fat and high in fibre, fruit makes the ultimate guilt-free snack – a handful of grapes, a banana or an apple can revitalize in moments, providing instant energy.

Left: A handful of grapes makes a perfect guilt-free snack that will provide your body with vital energy.

Raw fruits can be used in a huge number of ways: simply sliced into wedges and served with mild or strongly-flavoured cheese, cut into bite-size chunks for a fruit salad, macerated with a liqueur as a simple dessert to serve with ice cream, or puréed to make a vibrant and mouth-watering sauce. In fact, purées of both raw and cooked fruits form the basis of an enormous range of fruit desserts, from ice creams and sorbets to creamy mousses and soufflés.

Below: Perfectly ripe melons need little more than a spoonful or two of ginger syrup to set off their flavour in an eye-catching and refreshing fruit salad.

Whole fresh fruits, such as raspberries, strawberries, blueberries and black-currants, are delicious on their own or combined with other fruits. They can be used to fill crisp, golden pastry cases or piled high on top of a cream-filled pavlova shell.

Once you start to cook with fruits, their versatility really comes to light. There are so many different ways to bring out their flavours and alter their textures: they can be made into all manner of pies and tarts, baked under crumble toppings, filled with nutty stuffings and grilled, or poached in light flavoured syrups to serve on their own or use as a pie filling.

The flavours and textures of most fruits complement each other, giving the freedom to create all sorts of exciting sweet and savoury combinations. The majority of recipes in this book concentrate on the sweeter side of things, but fruits can also make an invaluable addition to savoury dishes. Sharp and acidic fruits, such as gooseberries, rhubarb and cranberries, cut through the richness of fatty fish, such as mackerel, and can enhance the subtle flavour of poultry, such as turkey and chicken. Dried fruits are used extensively in North African and Middle Eastern cooking and are a popular ingredient in savoury dishes. The combination of sweet prunes, dates or dried apricots with savoury stews and casseroles is superb. Often these sweet/savoury dishes are highly spiced

Introduction 7

as the flavours of fruits and spices marry well, complementing their distinctive tastes and aromas.

There are many hundreds of different types of fruit, which can be divided into four main categories: soft fruits, such as raspberries, strawberries, blueberries and red-, black- and whitecurrants; stone fruits, including peaches, apricots, cherries and plums; "pome" fruits of the apple and pear families; and citrus fruits. In addition there are the "one-offs" that do not fit into any of these categories. These one-offs include figs, grapes, melons and rhubarb.

Enjoying fruit was once tied to the season but nowadays, thanks to sophisticated transportation and improved farming methods, all types of fruit from every country are available almost all year round. Travellers who have enjoyed exotic produce abroad now find it gracing the shelves of their local greengrocer or supermarket.

The disadvantage of this is that we no longer wait with eager anticipation for a particular fruit to come into season; somewhere in the world it will be grown year-round. So fresh strawberries and peaches have ceased to be exclusively summer treats, but can be bought in almost any season, although they will never taste as good as when freshly picked, and are still always at their best in the summer.

Above: Succulent summer berries look wonderful and taste divine piled high on top of desserts, such as pavlovas

Below: Stone fruits, such as nectarines, are delicious eaten raw but they are equally good in many cooked fruit dishes.

There are many other ways of savouring fruits throughout the year. They can be frozen, bottled or preserved in other ways – as juices or liqueurs or macerated in alcohol; canned, dried or candied; or made into jams, jellies, curds and chutneys.

This wonderful collection of recipes will help you to make the most of fruit. The recipes are divided into six easy-to-use chapters. Each is devoted to a specific family of fruit: apples, pears and quinces; stone fruit; berries and currants, citrus fruit; exotic fruit; and finally those hard to classify fruits – melons, grapes, figs and rhubarb. Every chapter offers an inspiring choice, from the simplest fruit salads to more complicated pastries and desserts, plus a selection of sweet and savoury preserves. Whatever your mood, whether it's for refreshing Blackcurrant Sorbet, a comforting bowl of Spiced Apple Crumble, or indulgent Chocolate and Mandarin Truffle Slice, you are sure to find the perfect dish.

Apple, Pear and Quince Recipes

Apples, pears and quinces are wonderfully versatile. Dutch Apple Cake and Chocolate, Pear and Pecan Pie are just two of the tempting teatime treats in store, while Hot Quince Soufflés and Tarte Tatin make memorable desserts.

SPICED APPLE CRUMBLE

ANY FRUIT CAN BE USED IN THIS POPULAR DESSERT, BUT YOU CAN'T BEAT THE FAVOURITES OF BLACKBERRY AND APPLE. HAZELNUTS AND CARDAMOM SEEDS GIVE THE TOPPING EXTRA FLAVOUR.

SERVES FOUR TO SIX

INGREDIENTS
- butter, for greasing
- 450g/1lb Bramley apples
- 115g/4oz/1 cup blackberries
- grated rind and juice of 1 orange
- 50g/2oz/⅓ cup light muscovado sugar
- custard, to serve

For the topping
- 175g/6oz/1½ cups plain flour
- 75g/3oz/⅓ cup butter
- 75g/3oz/⅓ cup caster sugar
- 25g/1oz/¼ cup chopped hazelnuts
- 2.5ml/½ tsp crushed cardamom seeds

VARIATIONS
This wonderfully good-natured pudding can be made with all sorts of fruit. Try plums, apricots, peaches or pears, alone or in combination with apples. Rhubarb makes a delectable crumble, especially when partnered with bananas.

1 Preheat the oven to 200°C/400°F/Gas 6. Generously butter a 1.2 litre/2 pint/5 cup baking dish. Peel and core the apples, then slice them into the prepared baking dish. Level the surface, then scatter the blackberries over. Sprinkle the orange rind and light muscovado sugar evenly over the top, then pour over the orange juice. Set the fruit mixture aside while you make the crumble topping.

2 Make the topping. Sift the flour into a bowl and rub in the butter until the mixture resembles coarse breadcrumbs. Stir in the caster sugar, hazelnuts and cardamom seeds. Scatter the topping over the top of the fruit.

3 Press the topping around the edges of the dish to seal in the juices. Bake for 30–35 minutes or until the crumble is golden. Serve hot, with custard.

BAKED STUFFED APPLES

THIS TRADITIONAL APPLE DESSERT IS EXCEPTIONALLY SIMPLE AND SPEEDY. BAKE THE APPLES IN THE OVEN ON THE SHELF UNDER THE SUNDAY ROAST FOR A DELICIOUS END TO THE MEAL.

SERVES FOUR

INGREDIENTS
- 4 large Bramley apples
- 75g/3oz/½ cup light muscovado sugar
- 75g/3oz/⅓ cup butter, softened
- grated rind and juice of ½ orange
- 1.5ml/¼ tsp ground cinnamon
- 30ml/2 tbsp crushed ratafia biscuits
- 50g/2oz/½ cup pecan nuts, chopped
- 50g/2oz/½ cup luxury mixed glacé fruit, chopped

COOK'S TIP
Use a little butter or oil to grease the baking dish, if you like, or pour a small amount of water around the stuffed apples to stop them from sticking to the dish during baking.

1 Preheat the oven to 180°C/350°F/Gas 4. Wash and dry the apples. Remove the cores with an apple corer, then carefully enlarge each core cavity to twice its size, by shaving off more flesh with the corer. Score each apple around its equator, using a sharp knife. Stand the apples in a baking dish.

2 Mix the sugar, butter, orange rind and juice, cinnamon and ratafia crumbs. Beat well, then stir in the nuts and glacé fruit. Divide the filling among the apples, piling it high. Shield the filling in each apple with a small piece of foil. Bake for 45–60 minutes until each apple is tender.

Apple Crêpes with Butterscotch Sauce

These wonderful dessert crêpes are flavoured with sweet cider, filled with caramelized apples and drizzled with a rich, smooth butterscotch sauce.

3 Make the filling. Core the apples and cut them into thick slices. Heat 15g/½ oz/1 tbsp of the butter in a large frying pan. Add the apples to the pan. Cook until golden on both sides, then transfer the slices to a bowl with a slotted spoon and set them aside.

SERVES FOUR

INGREDIENTS
   115g/4oz/1 cup plain flour
   pinch of salt
   2 eggs
   175ml/6fl oz/¾ cup creamy milk
   120ml/4fl oz/½ cup sweet cider
   butter, for frying
For the filling and sauce
   4 Braeburn apples
   90g/3½ oz/scant ½ cup butter
   225g/8oz/1⅓ cups light
     muscovado sugar
   150ml/¼ pint/⅔ cup double cream

1 Make the crêpe batter. Sift the flour and salt into a large bowl. Add the eggs and milk and beat until smooth. Stir in the cider; set aside for 30 minutes.

2 Heat a small heavy-based non-stick frying pan. Add a knob of butter and ladle in enough batter to coat the pan thinly. Cook until the crêpe is golden underneath, then flip it over and cook the other side until golden. Slide the crêpe on to a plate. Repeat with the remaining mixture to make seven more.

4 Add the rest of the butter to the pan. As soon as it has melted, add the muscovado sugar. When the sugar has dissolved and the mixture is bubbling, stir in the cream. Continue cooking until it forms a smooth sauce.

5 Fold each pancake in half, then fold in half again to form a cone; fill each with some of the fried apples. Place two filled pancakes on each dessert plate, drizzle over some of the butterscotch sauce and serve at once.

VARIATIONS
You could just as easily use plums, pears, strawberries or bananas to fill the crêpes. If you like, add a touch of Grand Marnier to the apples towards the end of cooking.

Apple, Pear and Quince Recipes 13

Pear and Cinnamon Fritters

If you don't like deep frying as a rule, do make an exception for this dish. Fritters are irresistible, and a wonderful way of persuading children to eat more fruit.

SERVES FOUR

INGREDIENTS
- 3 ripe, firm pears
- 30ml/2 tbsp caster sugar
- 30ml/2 tbsp Kirsch
- groundnut oil, for frying
- 50g/2oz/1 cup amaretti biscuits, finely crushed

For the batter
- 75g/3oz/¾ cup plain flour
- 1.5ml/¼ tsp salt
- 1.5ml/¼ tsp ground cinnamon
- 60ml/4 tbsp milk
- 2 eggs, separated
- 45ml/3 tbsp water

To serve
- 30ml/2 tbsp caster sugar
- 1.5ml/¼ tsp ground cinnamon
- clotted cream

1 Peel the pears, cut them in quarters and remove the cores. Toss the wedges in the caster sugar and Kirsch. Set aside for 15 minutes.

2 Make the batter. Sift the flour, salt and cinnamon into a large bowl. Beat in the milk, egg yolks and water until smooth. Set aside for 10 minutes.

3 Whisk the egg whites in a grease-free bowl until they form stiff peaks; lightly fold them into the batter. Preheat the oven to 150°C/300°F/Gas 2.

4 Pour oil into a deep heavy-based saucepan to a depth of 7.5cm/3in. Heat to 185°C/360°F or until a bread cube, added to the oil, browns in 45 seconds.

5 Toss a pear wedge in the amaretti crumbs, then spear it on a fork and dip it into the batter until evenly coated. Lower it gently into the hot oil and use a knife to push it off the fork. Add more wedges in the same way but do not overcrowd the pan. Cook the fritters for 3–4 minutes or until golden. Drain on kitchen paper. Keep hot in the oven while cooking successive batches.

6 Mix the sugar and cinnamon and sprinkle some over the fritters. Sprinkle a little cinnamon sugar over the clotted cream; serve with the hot fritters.

VARIATIONS
Also try apples, apricots and bananas.

Poached Pears in Port Syrup

The perfect choice for autumn entertaining, this simple dessert has a beautiful rich colour and fantastic flavour thanks to the tastes of port and lemon.

SERVES FOUR

INGREDIENTS
- 2 ripe, firm pears, such as Williams or Comice
- pared rind of 1 lemon
- 175ml/6fl oz/¾ cup ruby port
- 50g/2oz/¼ cup caster sugar
- 1 cinnamon stick
- 60ml/4 tbsp cold water
- fresh cream, to serve

To decorate
- 30ml/2 tbsp sliced hazelnuts, toasted
- fresh mint, pear or rose leaves

COOK'S TIP
Choose pears of similar size, with the stalks intact, for the most attractive effect when fanned on the plate.

1 Peel the pears, cut them in half and remove the cores. Place the lemon rind, port, sugar, cinnamon stick and water in a shallow pan. Bring to the boil over a low heat. Add the pears, lower the heat, cover and poach for 5 minutes. Let the pears cool in the syrup.

2 When the pears are cold, transfer them to a bowl with a slotted spoon. Return the syrup to the heat. Boil rapidly until it has reduced to form a syrup that will coat the back of a spoon lightly. Remove the cinnamon stick and lemon rind and leave the syrup to cool.

3 To serve, place each pear in turn on a board, cut side down. Keeping it intact at the stalk end, slice it lengthways, then using a palette knife, carefully lift it off and place on a dessert plate. Press gently so that the pear fans out. When all the pears have been fanned, spoon over the port syrup. Top each portion with a few hazelnuts and decorate with fresh mint, pear or rose leaves. Serve with cream.

APPLE CHARLOTTES

THESE TEMPTING LITTLE FRUIT CHARLOTTES ARE A WONDERFUL WAY TO USE WINDFALLS.

SERVES FOUR

INGREDIENTS

- 175g/6oz/¾ cup butter
- 450g/1lb Bramley apples
- 225g/8oz Braeburn apples
- 60ml/4 tbsp water
- 130g/4½oz/scant ⅔ cup caster sugar
- 2 egg yolks
- pinch of grated nutmeg
- 9 thin slices white bread, crusts removed
- extra-thick double cream or custard, to serve

COOK'S TIP

A mixture of cooking and eating apples gives the best flavour, but there's no reason why you can't use only cooking apples; just sweeten the pulp to taste.

1 Preheat the oven to 190°C/375°F/Gas 5. Put a knob of the butter in a saucepan. Peel and core the apples, dice them finely and put them in the pan with the water. Cover and cook for 10 minutes or until the cooking apples have pulped down. Stir in 115g/4oz/½ cup of the caster sugar. Boil, uncovered, until any liquid has evaporated and what remains is a thick pulp. Remove from the heat, beat in the egg yolks and nutmeg and set aside.

2 Melt the remaining butter in a separate saucepan over a low heat until the white curds start to separate from the clear yellow liquid. Remove from the heat. Leave to stand for a few minutes, then strain the clear clarified butter through a muslin-lined sieve.

3 Brush four 150ml/¼ pint/⅔ cup individual charlotte moulds or pudding tins with a little of the clarified butter; sprinkle with the remaining caster sugar. Cut the bread slices into 2.5cm/1in strips. Dip the strips into the remaining clarified butter; use to line the moulds or tins. Overlap the strips on the base to give the effect of a swirl and let the excess bread overhang the tops of the moulds or tins.

4 Fill each bread case with apple pulp. Fold the excess bread over the top of each mould or tin to make a lid; press down lightly. Bake for 45–50 minutes or until golden. Run a knife between each charlotte and its mould or tin, then turn out on to dessert plates. Serve with extra-thick double cream or custard.

Hot Quince Soufflés

THESE DELICIOUS FRUITS ARE MORE OFTEN PICKED THAN PURCHASED AS THEY ARE SELDOM FOUND IN SHOPS OR MARKETS. YOU CAN USE PEARS INSTEAD, BUT THE FLAVOUR WILL NOT BE AS INTENSE.

SERVES SIX

INGREDIENTS
  2 quinces, peeled and cored
  60ml/4 tbsp water
  115g/4oz/½ cup caster sugar, plus extra for sprinkling
  5 egg whites
  melted butter, for greasing
  icing sugar, for dusting
For the pastry cream
  250ml/8fl oz/1 cup milk
  1 vanilla pod
  3 egg yolks
  75g/3oz/⅓ cup caster sugar
  25g/1oz/¼ cup plain flour
  15ml/1 tbsp Poire William liqueur

1 Cut the quinces into cubes. Place in a saucepan with the water. Stir in half the sugar. Bring to the boil, lower the heat, cover and simmer for 10 minutes or until tender. Remove the lid; boil until most of the liquid has evaporated.

2 Cool slightly, then purée the fruit in a blender or food processor. Press through a sieve into a bowl; set aside.

3 Make the pastry cream. Pour the milk into a small saucepan. Add the vanilla pod and bring to the boil over a low heat. Meanwhile, beat the egg yolks, caster sugar and flour in a bowl until smooth.

4 Gradually strain the hot milk on to the yolks, whisking frequently until the mixture is smooth.

5 Discard the vanilla pod. Return the mixture to the clean pan and heat gently, stirring until thickened. Cook, for a further 2 minutes, whisking constantly, to ensure that the sauce is smooth and the flour is cooked.

6 Remove the pan from the heat and stir in the quince purée and liqueur. Cover the surface of the pastry cream with clear film to prevent it from forming a skin. Allow to cool slightly, while you prepare the ramekins.

7 Preheat the oven to 220°C/425°F/Gas 7. Place a baking sheet in the oven to heat up. Butter six 150ml/¼ pint/⅔ cup ramekins and sprinkle the inside of each with caster sugar. In a grease-free bowl, whisk the egg whites to stiff peaks. Gradually whisk in the remaining caster sugar, then fold the egg whites into the pastry cream.

8 Divide the mixture among the prepared ramekins and level the surface of each. Carefully run a sharp knife between the side of each ramekin and the mixture, then place the ramekins on the hot baking sheet and bake for 8–10 minutes until the tops of the soufflés are well risen and golden. Generously dust the tops with icing sugar and serve the soufflés at once.

COOK'S TIP
Poire William is a clear, colourless pear eau-de-vie, which sometimes is sold with a ripe pear in the bottle. Kirsch, made from cherries, also works well in this recipe to complement the flavour of the quinces.

18 Apple, Pear and Quince Recipes

Tarte Tatin

If you use ready-rolled puff pastry, this tasty tart can be made very easily.

SERVES SIX TO EIGHT

INGREDIENTS
   3 Braeburn or Cox's Orange
     Pippin apples
   juice of ½ lemon
   50g/2oz/¼ cup butter, softened
   75g/3oz/⅓ cup caster sugar
   250g/9oz ready-rolled puff pastry
   cream, to serve

1 Preheat the oven to 220°C/425°F/Gas 7. Cut the apples in quarters and remove the cores. Toss the apple quarters in the lemon juice to prevent them discolouring.

2 Spread the butter over the base of a 20cm/8in heavy-based omelette pan that can safely be used in the oven. Sprinkle the caster sugar over the base of the pan and add the apple wedges, rounded side down.

3 Cook over a medium heat for 15–20 minutes or until the sugar and butter have melted and the apples are golden. Cut the pastry into a 25cm/10in round and place on top of the apples; tuck the edges in with a knife. Place the pan in the oven and bake for 15–20 minutes or until the pastry is golden. Carefully invert the tart on to a plate. Cool slightly before serving with cream.

COOK'S TIP
To turn out the Tarte Tatin, place the serving plate upside down on top of it, then, protecting your arms with oven gloves, hold both pan and plate firmly together and deftly turn them over. Lift off the pan.

Apple, Pear and Quince Recipes 19

FILO-TOPPED APPLE PIE

WITH ITS SCRUNCHY FILO TOPPING AND MINIMAL BUTTER, THIS MAKES A REALLY LIGHT DESSERT. A GOOD CHOICE FOR THE APPLE PIE ADDICT WATCHING HIS OR HER FAT INTAKE.

SERVES SIX

INGREDIENTS
- 900g/2lb Bramley apples
- 75g/3oz/⅓ cup caster sugar
- grated rind of 1 lemon
- 15ml/1 tbsp lemon juice
- 75g/3oz/½ cup sultanas
- 2.5ml/½ tsp ground cinnamon
- 4 large sheets filo pastry, thawed if frozen
- 25g/1oz/2 tbsp butter, melted
- icing sugar, for dusting

VARIATION
To make filo crackers, cut the buttered filo into 20cm/8in wide strips. Spoon a little of the filling along one end of each strip, leaving the sides clear. Roll up and twist the ends to make a cracker. Brush with more butter; bake for 20 minutes.

1 Peel, core and dice the apples. Place them in a saucepan with the caster sugar and lemon rind. Drizzle the lemon juice over. Bring to the boil, stir well, then cook for 5 minutes or until the apples have softened. Stir in the sultanas and cinnamon. Spoon the mixture into a 1.2 litre/2 pint/5 cup pie dish and level the top. Allow to cool.

2 Preheat the oven to 180°C/350°F/Gas 4. Place a pie funnel in the centre of the fruit. Brush each sheet of filo with melted butter. Scrunch up loosely and place on the fruit to cover it completely.

3 Bake for 20–30 minutes until the filo is golden. Dust the pie with icing sugar before serving with custard or cream.

CHOCOLATE, PEAR AND PECAN PIE

THE RICHNESS OF DEEP, DARK CHOCOLATE COUPLED WITH JUICY PEARS GIVES A CLASSIC PECAN PIE AN OUT-OF-THE-ORDINARY TWIST. THE RESULT IS UTTERLY DELICIOUS — AND UTTERLY IRRESISTIBLE.

SERVES EIGHT TO TEN

INGREDIENTS

   300g/11oz shortcrust pastry, thawed if frozen
   3 small pears
   165g/5½oz/scant ¾ cup caster sugar
   150ml/¼ pint/⅔ cup water
   pared rind of 1 lemon
   50g/2oz good quality plain chocolate
   50g/2oz/¼ cup unsalted butter, diced
   225g/8oz/¾ cup golden syrup
   3 eggs, beaten
   5ml/1 tsp pure vanilla essence
   150g/5oz/1¼ cups pecan nuts, chopped
   15ml/1 tbsp maple syrup (optional)
   ice cream, to serve

1 Preheat the oven to 200°C/400°F/Gas 6. Roll out the pastry on a lightly floured surface and line a deep 23cm/9in fluted flan tin. Chill the pastry case for 20 minutes, then line it with non-stick baking paper and baking beans. Bake for 10 minutes. Lift out the paper and beans and return the pastry case to the oven for 5 minutes. Allow to cool.

2 Peel the pears, cut them in half and remove the cores with a small spoon. Place 50g/2oz/¼ cup of the sugar in a pan with the water. Add the lemon rind and bring to the boil. Add the pears. Cover, lower the heat and simmer for 10 minutes. Remove the pears from the pan with a slotted spoon and set aside to cool. Discard the cooking liquid.

3 Break the chocolate into a large heatproof bowl. Melt over a pan of barely simmering water. Beat in the butter until combined. Set aside. In a saucepan, heat the remaining sugar and golden syrup together over a low heat until most of the sugar has dissolved. Bring to the boil, lower the heat and simmer for 2 minutes.

4 Whisk the eggs into the chocolate mixture until combined, then whisk in the syrup mixture. Stir in the vanilla essence and pecan nuts.

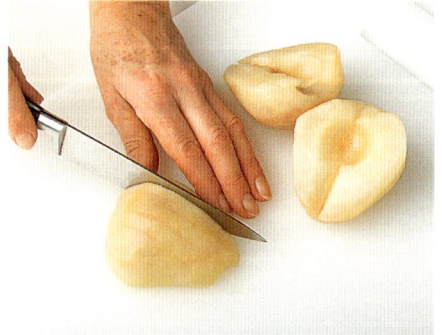

5 Place the pear halves flat side down on a board. Using a fine sharp knife, make lengthways cuts all along each pear, taking care not to cut all the way through. Using a palette knife, lift the pear halves and arrange in the pastry case. Pour the pecan mixture over the top, so that the pears are visible through the mixture.

6 Bake for 25–30 minutes or until the filling is set, then allow to cool on a wire rack. If you like, glaze the surface of the pie with maple syrup before serving with ice cream.

French Apple Tart

This glorious tart makes a truly indulgent dessert. For an early morning treat, try a slice for breakfast with a cup of strong black coffee.

SERVES EIGHT

INGREDIENTS
 350g/12oz sweet shortcrust pastry, thawed if frozen
 whipped cream, to serve
For the filling
 115g/4oz/½ cup butter, softened
 115g/4oz/½ cup caster sugar
 2 large eggs, beaten
 115g/4oz/1 cup ground almonds
 25g/1oz/¼ cup plain flour
For the topping
 3 Braeburn apples
 60ml/4 tbsp apricot jam
 15ml/1 tbsp water

1 Preheat the oven to 190°C/375°F/Gas 5. Place a baking sheet in the oven to heat up. Roll out the shortcrust pastry on a lightly floured surface and line a 23cm/9in fluted flan tin.

4 Using a palette knife, carefully transfer each row of apple slices to the tart, arranging them on the filling so that they resemble the spokes of a wheel. You may need to overlap the slices in the middle slightly to fit. Press the slices down well into the filling. Warm the apricot jam with the water, then press the mixture through a sieve into a small bowl.

5 Using a pastry brush, brush half this jam glaze over the apples. Place the tin on the hot baking sheet and bake the tart for 45 minutes or until the pastry is golden and the apples have started to singe slightly.

6 Warm the remaining jam glaze and brush it over the apples. Let the tart cool slightly before serving with cream.

2 Beat all the ingredients for the filling together until light and fluffy. Spoon into the pastry case and level the surface.

3 Make the topping. Peel the apples, remove the cores, and cut them in half. Place each half, cut side down, on a board. Using a sharp, fine knife, slice the apples thinly, keeping the shape, then press down lightly to fan each apple half in a row.

VARIATION
A redcurrant glaze would also look good on this tart. Warm redcurrant jelly with a little lemon juice and brush it over the apples. Sieving is not needed.

DUTCH APPLE CAKE

THE APPLE TOPPING MAKES THIS CAKE REALLY MOIST. IT IS JUST AS GOOD HOT AS IT IS COLD.

MAKES EIGHT TO TEN SLICES

INGREDIENTS
- 250g/9oz/2¼ cups self-raising flour
- 10ml/2 tsp baking powder
- 5ml/1 tsp ground cinnamon
- 130g/4½oz/generous ½ cup caster sugar
- 50g/2oz/¼ cup butter, melted
- 2 eggs, beaten
- 150ml/¼ pint/⅔ cup milk

For the topping
- 2 Cox's Orange Pippin apples
- 15g/½oz/1 tbsp butter, melted
- 60ml/4 tbsp demerara sugar
- 1.5ml/¼ tsp ground cinnamon

VARIATION
Add a few sultanas or raisins to the apples if you like.

1 Preheat the oven to 200°C/400°F/Gas 6. Grease and line a 20cm/8in round cake tin. Sift the flour, baking powder and cinnamon into a large mixing bowl. Stir in the caster sugar. In a separate bowl, whisk the melted butter, eggs and milk together, then stir the mixture into the dry ingredients.

2 Pour the cake mixture into the prepared tin, smooth the surface, then make a shallow hollow in a ring around the edge of the mixture.

3 Make the topping. Peel and core the apples, slice them into wedges and slice the wedges thinly. Arrange the slices around the hollow of the cake mixture. Brush with the melted butter, then scatter the demerara sugar and ground cinnamon over the top.

4 Bake for 45–50 minutes or until the cake has risen well, is golden and a skewer inserted into the centre comes out clean. Serve immediately as a dessert with cream, or remove from the tin, peel off the lining paper and cool on a wire rack before slicing.

PEAR AND POLENTA CAKE

POLENTA GIVES THE LIGHT SPONGE THAT TOPS SLICED PEARS A NUTTY CORN FLAVOUR THAT COMPLEMENTS THE FRUIT PERFECTLY. SERVE AS A DESSERT WITH CUSTARD OR CREAM.

MAKES TEN SLICES

INGREDIENTS
- 175g/6oz/¾ cup golden caster sugar
- 4 ripe pears
- juice of ½ lemon
- 30ml/2 tbsp clear honey
- 3 eggs
- seeds from 1 vanilla pod
- 120ml/4fl oz/½ cup sunflower oil
- 115g/4oz/1 cup self-raising flour
- 50g/2oz/⅓ cup instant polenta

1 Preheat the oven to 180°C/350°F/Gas 4. Generously grease and line a 21cm/8½in round cake tin. Scatter 30ml/2 tbsp of the golden caster sugar over the base of the prepared tin.

COOK'S TIP
Use the tip of a small, sharp knife to scrape out the vanilla pod seeds. If you do not have a vanilla pod, use 5ml/1 tsp pure vanilla essence instead.

2 Peel and core the pears. Cut them into chunky slices and toss in the lemon juice. Arrange them on the base of the prepared cake tin. Drizzle the honey over the pears and set aside.

3 Mix together the eggs, seeds from the vanilla pod and the remaining golden caster sugar in a bowl.

4 Beat the egg mixture until thick and creamy, then gradually beat in the oil. Sift together the flour and polenta and fold into the egg mixture.

5 Pour the mixture carefully into the tin over the pears. Bake for about 50 minutes or until a skewer inserted into the centre comes out clean. Cool in the tin for 10 minutes, then turn the cake out on to a plate, peel off the lining paper, invert and slice.

APPLE AND CIDER SAUCE

THIS SAUCE COULDN'T BE SIMPLER TO MAKE. IT TASTES GREAT WITH ROAST PORK, DUCK OR GOOSE.

MAKES 450G/1LB

INGREDIENTS
- 450g/1lb Bramley apples
- 150ml/¼ pint/⅔ cup sweet cider
- 2.5ml/½ tsp cider vinegar
- 25g/1oz/2 tbsp butter
- 2 whole cloves
- a few sprigs of fresh thyme
- 15ml/1 tbsp clear honey
- 2 tsp Dijon mustard

1 Peel, core and slice the apples. Place them in a saucepan with the cider, cider vinegar, butter, cloves and thyme. Simmer over a low heat for 10 minutes or until the apples are soft and pulpy, stirring occasionally, then raise the heat and cook until most of the liquid has evaporated.

2 Remove the cloves and thyme sprigs and beat in the honey and mustard. Taste and add more honey if necessary, but the sauce is best when slightly tart.

COOK'S TIP
Press the sauce through a sieve if you prefer it to be perfectly smooth.

APPLE AND RED ONION MARMALADE

THIS MARMALADE CHUTNEY IS GOOD ENOUGH TO EAT ON ITS OWN. SERVE IT WITH GOOD PORK SAUSAGES FOR THOROUGHLY MODERN HOT DOGS OR IN A HAM SANDWICH INSTEAD OF MUSTARD.

MAKES 450G/1LB

INGREDIENTS
- 60ml/4 tbsp extra virgin olive oil
- 900g/2lb red onions, thinly sliced
- 75g/3oz/½ cup demerara sugar
- 2 Cox's Orange Pippin apples
- 90ml/6 tbsp cider vinegar

1 Heat the oil in a large, heavy-based saucepan and add the onions.

2 Stir in the sugar and cook, uncovered, over a medium heat for about 40 minutes, stirring occasionally, or until the onions have softened and become a rich golden colour.

3 Peel, core and grate the apples. Add them to the pan with the vinegar and continue to cook for 20 minutes until the chutney is thick and sticky. Spoon into a sterilized jar and cover.

4 When cool, label and store in the fridge for up to 1 month.

STONE FRUIT RECIPES

Juicy and full of flavour, peaches, plums, apricots, cherries and nectarines make perfect partners for crisp pastry. Try the irresistible Baked Lattice Peaches or Plum and Marzipan Pastries. For simpler, but equally delicious desserts, plump for Peach Melba Syllabub or Nectarine and Hazelnut Meringues.

Peach Melba Syllabub

If you are making these sophisticated temptations for a dinner party, cook the peaches and raspberries the day before to allow the fruit to chill. Whip up the syllabub at the very last minute to make a delicious, light-as-a-cloud topping.

SERVES SIX

INGREDIENTS
4 peaches, peeled, stoned and sliced
300ml/½ pint/1¼ cups blush or red grape juice
115g/4oz/⅔ cup raspberries
raspberry or mint leaves, to decorate
ratafias or other dessert biscuits, to serve
For the syllabub
   60ml/4 tbsp peach schnapps
   30ml/2 tbsp blush or red grape juice
   300ml/½ pint/1¼ cups double cream

VARIATIONS
Use dessert pears and sliced kiwi fruit instead of peaches and raspberries. Instead of the syllabub, top the fruit with whipped cream flavoured with Advocaat and finely chopped preserved ginger.

1 Place the peach slices in a large saucepan. Add the grape juice. Bring to the boil, then cover, lower the heat and simmer for 5–7 minutes or until tender.

2 Add the raspberries and remove from the heat. Set aside in the fridge until cold. Divide the peach and raspberry mixture among six dessert glasses.

3 For the syllabub, place the peach schnapps and grape juice in a large bowl and whisk in the cream until it forms soft peaks.

4 Spoon the syllabub on top of the fruit and decorate each portion with a fresh raspberry or mint leaf. Serve with ratafias or other dessert biscuits.

Nectarine and Hazelnut Meringues

If it's indulgence you're seeking, look no further. Sweet nectarines and cream syllabub paired with crisp hazelnut meringues make a superb sweet.

SERVES FIVE

INGREDIENTS
3 egg whites
175g/6oz/¾ cup caster sugar
50g/2oz/½ cup chopped hazelnuts, toasted
300ml/½ pint/1¼ cups double cream
60ml/4 tbsp sweet dessert wine
2 nectarines, stoned and sliced
fresh mint sprigs, to decorate

VARIATIONS
Use apricots instead of nectarines if you prefer, or try this with a raspberry filling.

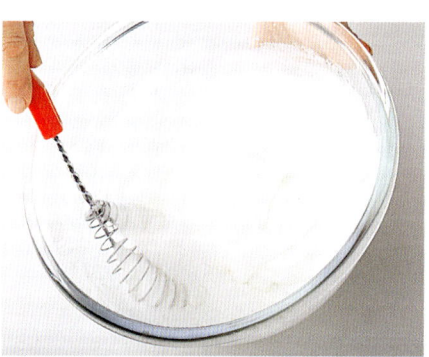

1 Preheat the oven to 140°C/275°F/Gas 1. Line two large baking sheets with non-stick baking paper. Whisk or beat the egg whites in a grease-free bowl until they form stiff peaks when the whisk or beaters are lifted. Gradually whisk in the caster sugar a spoonful at a time until the mixture forms a stiff, glossy meringue.

2 Fold in two thirds of the chopped toasted hazelnuts, then spoon five large ovals on to each lined baking sheet. Scatter the remaining hazelnuts over five of the meringue ovals. Flatten the tops of the remaining five ovals.

3 Bake the meringues for 1–1¼ hours until crisp and dry, then carefully lift them off the baking paper and cool completely on a wire rack.

4 Whip the cream with the dessert wine until the mixture forms soft peaks. Spoon some of the cream syllabub on to each of the plain meringues. Arrange a few nectarine slices on each. Put each meringue on a dessert plate with a hazelnut-topped meringue. Decorate each portion with mint sprigs and serve the meringues immediately.

Black Cherry Clafoutis

This favourite recipe has been reproduced with all manner of fruit, but you simply can't beat the classic version using slightly tart black cherries.

SERVES SIX

INGREDIENTS

25g/1oz/2 tbsp butter, for greasing
450g/1lb/2 cups black cherries, stoned
25g/1oz/¼ cup plain flour
50g/2oz/½ cup icing sugar, plus extra for dusting
4 eggs, beaten
250ml/8fl oz/1 cup creamy milk
30ml/2 tbsp Kirsch

1 Preheat the oven to 180°C/350°F/Gas 4. Use the butter to thickly grease a 1.2 litre/2 pint/5 cup gratin dish. Scatter the cherries over the base.

2 Sift the flour and icing sugar together into a large mixing bowl and gradually whisk in the eggs until the mixture is smooth. Whisk in the milk until blended, then stir in the Kirsch.

3 Pour the batter carefully over the cherries, then bake for 35–45 minutes or until just set and lightly golden.

4 Allow the pudding to cool for about 15 minutes. Dust liberally with icing sugar just before serving.

VARIATIONS

Try other liqueurs in this dessert. Almond-flavoured liqueur is delicious teamed with cherries. Hazelnut, raspberry or orange liqueur would also work nicely.

Stone Fruit Recipes 31

ICED GIN AND DAMSON SOUFFLÉS

FOR AN UNFORGETTABLE TASTE SENSATION, USE SLOE GIN FOR THESE DELICIOUS INDIVIDUAL FROZEN SOUFFLÉS. THEY ARE PERFECT FOR A PARTY AND CAN BE MADE AHEAD.

MAKES SIX

INGREDIENTS
- 500g/1¼lb damsons
- 250ml/8fl oz/1 cup water
- 275g/10oz/1¼ cups caster sugar
- 30ml/2 tbsp gin or sloe gin
- 4 large egg whites
- 300ml/½ pint/1¼ cups double cream, whipped
- fresh mint leaves, to decorate

4 Meanwhile, whisk the egg whites in a grease-free bowl until they form stiff peaks. Still whisking, slowly pour in the hot syrup until the meringue mixture is stiff and glossy. Fold in the whipped cream and fruit purée until combined.

5 Spoon into the dishes to come 2.5cm/1in above the rim of each. Freeze until firm. Remove from the freezer 10 minutes before serving. Remove the collars, then decorate each with damson slices and mint leaves.

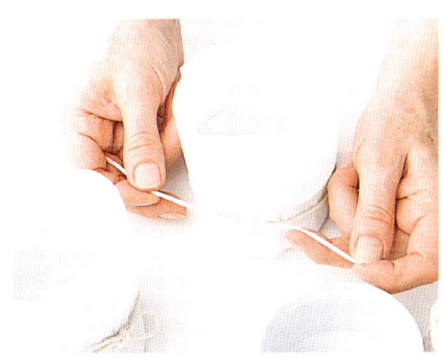

1 You will need six 150ml/¼ pint/⅔ cup ramekins. Give each a collar of greased non-stick baking paper that extends about 5cm/2in above the rim.

2 Slice two damsons and set aside for the decoration. Put the rest of the damsons in a pan with half the water and 50g/2oz/¼ cup of the caster sugar. Cover and simmer the mixture for about 7 minutes, or until the damsons are tender. Press the pulp through a sieve placed over a bowl to remove all the stones and skin, then stir in the gin and set aside.

3 Combine the remaining sugar and water in the clean pan and heat gently until the sugar has dissolved. Bring to the boil and cook the syrup until it registers 119°C/238°F on a sugar thermometer, or until a small amount of the mixture dropped into a cup of cold water can be moulded to a soft ball.

Caramelized Apricots with Pain Perdu

Pain perdu is a French invention that literally translates as "lost bread". Americans call it French toast, while a British version is known as Poor Knights.

SERVES FOUR

INGREDIENTS
  75g/3oz/6 tbsp unsalted
    butter, clarified
  450g/1lb apricots, stoned and
    thickly sliced
  115g/4oz/½ cup caster sugar
  150ml/¼ pint/⅔ cup double cream
  30ml/2 tbsp apricot brandy or brandy
For the pain perdu
  600ml/1 pint/2½ cups milk
  1 vanilla pod
  50g/2oz/¼ cup caster sugar
  4 large eggs, beaten
  115g/4oz/½ cup unsalted
    butter, clarified
  6 brioche slices, diagonally halved
  2.5ml/½ tsp ground cinnamon

1 Heat a heavy-based frying pan, then melt a quarter of the butter. Add the apricot slices and cook for 2–3 minutes until golden. Using a slotted spoon, transfer them to a bowl. Add the rest of the butter to the pan with the sugar and heat gently, stirring, until golden.

2 Pour in the cream and brandy and cook gently until the mixture forms a smooth sauce. Boil for 2–3 minutes until thickened, then pour the sauce over the apricots and set aside.

3 To make the pain perdu, pour the milk into a saucepan and add the vanilla pod and half the sugar. Heat gently until almost boiling, then set aside to cool.

4 Remove the vanilla pod and pour the flavoured milk into a shallow dish. Whisk in the eggs. Heat a sixth of the butter in the clean frying pan. Dip each slice of brioche in turn into the milk mixture, add it to the pan and fry until golden brown on both sides. Add the remaining butter as needed. As the pain perdu is cooked, remove the slices; keep hot.

5 Warm the apricot sauce and spoon it on to the pain perdu. Mix the remaining sugar with the cinnamon and sprinkle a little of the mixture over each portion.

COOK'S TIP
To clarify the butter, melt it in a small saucepan, then leave it to stand for a few minutes. Carefully pour the clear butter on the surface (the clarified butter) into a small bowl, leaving the milky solids behind in the pan.

Stone Fruit Recipes   33

Fresh Cherry AND Hazelnut Strudel

Serve this wonderful old-world treat as a warm dessert with custard, or allow it to cool and offer it as a scrumptious cake with afternoon tea or coffee.

SERVES SIX TO EIGHT

INGREDIENTS
- 75g/3oz/6 tbsp butter
- 90ml/6 tbsp light muscovado sugar
- 3 egg yolks
- grated rind of 1 lemon
- 1.5ml/¼ tsp grated nutmeg
- 250g/9oz/generous 1 cup ricotta cheese
- 8 large sheets filo pastry, thawed if frozen
- 75g/3oz ratafias, crushed
- 450g/1lb/2½ cups cherries, stoned
- 30ml/2 tbsp chopped hazelnuts
- icing sugar, for dusting
- crème fraîche, to serve

1 Preheat the oven to 190°C/375°F/Gas 5. Soften 15g/½oz/1 tbsp of the butter. Place it in a bowl and beat in the sugar and egg yolks until light and fluffy. Beat in the lemon rind, nutmeg and ricotta, then set aside.

2 Melt the remaining butter in a small pan. Working quickly, place a sheet of filo on a clean tea towel and brush it generously with melted butter. Place a second sheet on top and repeat the process. Continue until all the filo has been layered and buttered, reserving some of the melted butter.

3 Scatter the crushed ratafias over the top, leaving a 5cm/2in border around the outside. Spoon the ricotta mixture over the biscuits, spread it lightly to cover, then scatter over the cherries.

4 Fold in the filo pastry border and use the dish towel to carefully roll up the strudel, Swiss-roll style, beginning from one of the long sides of the pastry. Grease a baking sheet with the remaining melted butter.

5 Place the strudel on the baking sheet and scatter the hazelnuts over the surface. Bake for 35–40 minutes or until the strudel is golden and crisp. Dust with icing sugar and serve with a dollop of crème fraîche.

Baked Lattice Peaches

IF YOU WOULD RATHER USE NECTARINES FOR THE RECIPE, THERE'S NO NEED TO PEEL THEM FIRST.

MAKES SIX

INGREDIENTS
- 3 peaches
- juice of ½ lemon
- 75g/3oz/scant ½ cup white marzipan
- 375g/13oz ready-rolled puff pastry, thawed if frozen
- a large pinch of ground cinnamon
- beaten egg, to glaze
- caster sugar, for sprinkling

For the caramel sauce
- 50g/2oz/¼ cup caster sugar
- 30ml/2 tbsp cold water
- 150ml/¼ pint/⅔ cup double cream

1 Preheat the oven to 190°C/375°F/Gas 5. Place the peaches in a large bowl and pour over boiling water to cover. Leave for 60 seconds, then drain the peaches and peel off the skins. Toss the skinned fruit in the lemon juice to stop them going brown.

2 Divide the marzipan into six pieces and shape each to form a small round. Cut the peaches in half and remove their stones. Fill the stone cavity in each with a marzipan round.

3 Unroll the puff pastry and cut it in half. Set one half aside, then cut out six rounds from the rest, making each round slightly larger than a peach half. Sprinkle a little cinnamon on each pastry round, then place a peach half, marzipan side down, on the pastry.

4 Cut the remaining pastry into lattice pastry, using a special cutter if you have one. If not, simply cut small slits in rows all over the pastry, starting each row slightly lower than the last. Cut the lattice pastry into six equal squares.

COOK'S TIP
Take care when adding the cream to the hot caramel as the mixture is liable to spit. Pour it from a jug, protecting your hand with an oven glove, and use a long-handled wooden spoon for stirring.

5 Dampen the edges of the pastry rounds with a little water, then drape a lattice pastry square over each peach half. Press around the edge to seal, then trim off the excess pastry and decorate with small peach leaves made from the trimmings. Transfer the peach pastries to a baking sheet. Brush with the beaten egg and sprinkle with the caster sugar. Bake for 20 minutes or until the pastries are golden.

6 Meanwhile, make the caramel sauce. Heat the sugar with the water in a small pan until it dissolves. Bring to the boil and continue to boil until the syrup turns a dark golden brown. Stand back and add the cream. Heat gently, stirring until smooth. Serve the peach pastries with the sauce.

Peach and Redcurrant Tartlets

TART REDCURRANTS AND SWEET PEACHES MAKE A WINNING COMBINATION IN THESE SIMPLE TARTLETS.

MAKES FOUR

INGREDIENTS
- 25g/1oz/2 tbsp butter, melted
- 16 × 15cm/6in squares of filo pastry, thawed if frozen
- icing sugar, for dusting
- redcurrant sprigs, to decorate

For the filling
- 150ml/¼ pint/⅔ cup double cream
- 125g/4¼oz carton peach and mango fromage frais
- a few drops of pure vanilla essence
- 15ml/1 tbsp icing sugar, sifted

For the topping
- 2 peaches
- 50g/2oz/½ cup redcurrants

COOK'S TIP
To strip redcurrants from their stalks, pull the stalks through the tines of a fork.

1 Preheat the oven to 190°C/375°F/Gas 5. Use a little of the butter to grease four large bun tins or individual tartlet tins. Brush the pastry squares with butter, stack them in fours, then place in the tins to make four pastry cases.

2 Bake for 12–15 minutes until golden. Cool the filo cases on a wire rack.

3 Make the filling. Whip the cream to soft peaks, then lightly fold in the fromage frais, vanilla essence and icing sugar. Divide among the pastry cases.

4 Slice the peaches and fan them out on top of the filling, interspersing with a few redcurrants. Decorate with redcurrant sprigs and dust with icing sugar.

PLUM AND MARZIPAN PASTRIES

These Danish pastries can be made with any pitted fruit. Try apricots, cherries, damsons or greengages, adding a glaze made from clear honey or a complementary jam.

MAKES SIX

INGREDIENTS

- 375g/13oz ready-rolled puff pastry
- 90ml/6 tbsp plum jam
- 115g/4oz/½ cup white marzipan, coarsely grated
- 3 red plums, halved and stoned
- 1 egg, beaten
- 50g/2oz/½ cup flaked almonds

For the glaze
- 30ml/2 tbsp plum jam
- 15ml/1 tbsp water

1 Preheat the oven to 220°C/425°F/Gas 7. Unroll the pastry, cut it into six equal squares and place on one or two dampened baking sheets.

2 Spoon 15ml/1 tbsp jam into the centre of each pastry square. Divide the marzipan among them. Place half a plum, hollow-side down, on top of each marzipan mound.

3 Brush the edges of the pastry with beaten egg. Bring up the corners and press them together lightly, then open out the pastry corners at the top. Glaze the pastries with a little beaten egg, then press a sixth of the flaked almonds on each.

4 Bake the pastries for 20–25 minutes or until lightly golden.

5 Meanwhile, make the glaze by heating the jam and water in a small pan, stirring until smooth. Press the mixture through a sieve into a small bowl, then brush it over the tops of the pastries while they are still warm. Leave to cool on a wire rack.

Yellow Plum Tart

In this tart, glazed yellow plums sit atop a delectable almond filling in a crisp pastry shell. When they are in season, greengages make an excellent alternative to the plums.

SERVES EIGHT

INGREDIENTS
  175g/6oz/1½ cups plain flour
  pinch of salt
  75g/3oz/scant ½ cup butter, chilled
  30ml/2 tbsp caster sugar
  a few drops of pure vanilla essence
  45ml/3 tbsp iced water
  cream or custard, to serve
For the filling
  75g/3oz/⅓ cup caster sugar
  75g/3oz/scant ½ cup butter, softened
  75g/3oz/¾ cup ground almonds
  1 egg, beaten
  30ml/2 tbsp plain flour
  450g/1lb yellow plums or greengages,
    halved and stoned
For the glaze
  45ml/3 tbsp apricot jam, sieved
  15ml/1 tbsp water

1 Sift the flour and salt into a bowl, then rub in the chilled butter until the mixture resembles fine breadcrumbs. Stir in the caster sugar, vanilla essence and enough of the iced water to make a soft dough.

2 Knead the dough gently on a lightly floured surface until smooth, then wrap in clear film and chill for 10 minutes.

3 Preheat the oven to 200°C/400°F/Gas 6. Roll out the pastry and line a 23cm/9in fluted flan tin, allowing excess pastry to overhang the top. Prick the base with a fork and line with non-stick baking paper and baking beans.

4 Bake blind for 10 minutes, remove the paper and beans, then return the pastry case to the oven for 10 minutes. Remove and allow to cool. Trim off any excess pastry with a sharp knife.

5 To make the filling, whisk or beat together all the ingredients except the plums or greengages. Spread on the base of the pastry case. Arrange the plums or greengages on top, placing them cut side down. Make a glaze by heating the jam with the water. Stir well, then brush a little of the jam glaze over the top of the fruit.

6 Bake the tart for 50–60 minutes, until the almond filling is cooked and the plums or greengages are tender. Warm any remaining jam glaze and brush it over the top. Cut into slices and serve with cream or custard.

COOK'S TIP
Ceramic baking beans are ideal for baking blind, but any dried beans will do. You can use them over and over again, but make sure you keep them in a special jar, separate from the rest of your dried beans, as you cannot use them for conventional cooking.

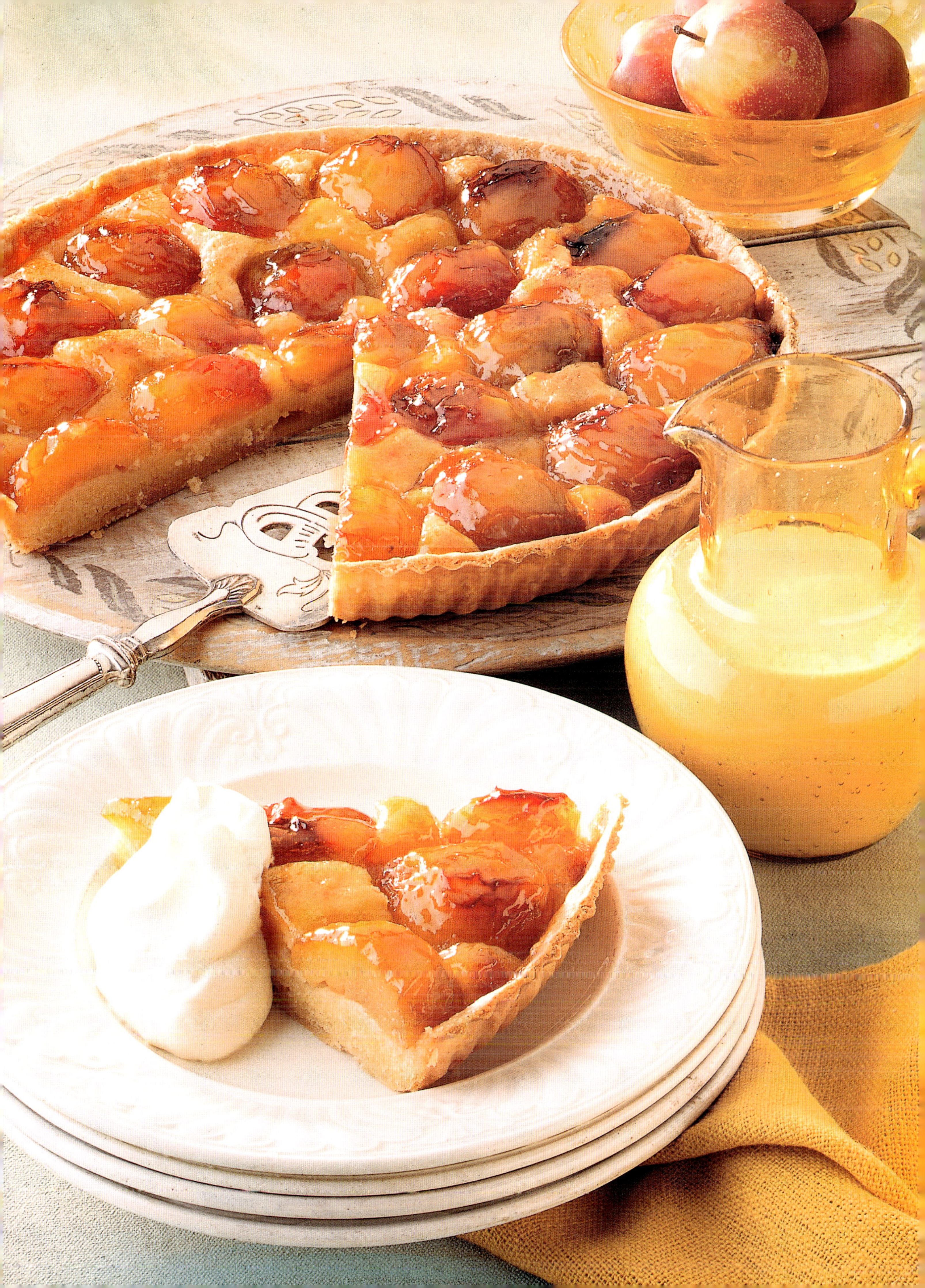

Apricot Parcels

These little filo parcels contain a special apricot and mincemeat filling. A good way to use up any mincemeat and marzipan that have been in your cupboard since Christmas!

MAKES EIGHT

INGREDIENTS

350g/12oz filo pastry, thawed if frozen
50g/2oz/¼ cup butter, melted
8 apricots, halved and stoned
60ml/4 tbsp luxury mincemeat
12 ratafias, crushed
30ml/2 tbsp grated marzipan
icing sugar, for dusting

COOK'S TIP
Filo pastry dries out quickly, so keep any squares not currently being used covered under a clean damp dish towel. Also, work as quickly as possible. If the filo should turn dry and brittle, simply brush it with melted butter to moisten.

1 Preheat the oven to 200°C/400°F/Gas 6. Cut the filo pastry into 32 × 18cm/7in squares. Brush four of the squares with a little melted butter and stack them, giving each layer a quarter turn so that the stack acquires a star shape. Repeat to make eight stars.

2 Place an apricot half, hollow up, in the centre of each pastry star. Mix together the mincemeat, crushed ratafias and marzipan and spoon a little of the mixture into the hollow in each apricot.

3 Top with another apricot half, then bring the corners of each pastry together and squeeze to make a gathered purse.

4 Place the purses on a baking sheet and brush each with a little melted butter. Bake for 15–20 minutes or until the pastry is golden and crisp. Lightly dust with icing sugar to serve. Whipped cream, flavoured with a little brandy, makes an ideal accompaniment.

Crunchy-topped Fresh Apricot Cake

Almonds are perfect partners for fresh apricots, and this is a great way to use up firm fruits. Serve cold as a cake or warm with custard for a dessert.

MAKES EIGHT SLICES

INGREDIENTS
175g/6oz/1½ cups self-raising flour
175g/6oz/¾ cup butter, softened
175g/6oz/¾ cup caster sugar
115g/4oz/1 cup ground almonds
3 eggs
5ml/1 tsp almond essence
2.5ml/½ tsp baking powder
8 firm apricots, stoned and chopped
For the topping
30ml/2 tbsp demerara sugar
50g/2oz/½ cup slivered almonds

1 Preheat the oven to 160°C/325°F/Gas 3. Grease an 18cm/7in round cake tin and line with non-stick baking paper. Put all the cake ingredients, except the apricots, in a large mixing bowl and whisk until creamy.

2 Fold the apricots into the cake mixture, then spoon into the prepared cake tin. Make a hollow in the centre with the back of a large spoon, then scatter 15ml/1 tbsp of the demerara sugar over for the topping, with the slivered almonds.

3 Bake for 1½ hours or until a skewer inserted into the middle comes out clean. Scatter the remaining demerara sugar over the top of the cake and leave to cool for 10 minutes in the tin. Remove from the tin, peel off the paper and finish cooling on a wire rack.

Pickled Peach and Chilli Chutney

This is a really spicy, rich chutney that is great served with cold roast meats such as ham, pork or turkey. It is also good with a strong farmhouse Cheddar cheese.

MAKES 450G/1LB

INGREDIENTS
  475ml/16fl oz/2 cups cider vinegar
  275g/10oz/1⅔ cups light muscovado sugar
  225g/8oz/1 cup dried dates, pitted and finely chopped
  5ml/1 tsp ground allspice
  5ml/1 tsp ground mace
  450g/1lb ripe peaches, stoned and cut into small chunks
  3 onions, thinly sliced
  4 fresh red chillies, seeded and finely chopped
  4 garlic cloves, crushed
  5cm/2in piece of fresh root ginger, finely grated
  5ml/1 tsp salt

1 Place the vinegar, sugar, dates and spices in a large saucepan and bring to the boil, stirring occasionally.

2 Add all the remaining ingredients and return to the boil. Lower the heat and simmer for 40–50 minutes or until thick. Stir often to prevent the mixture from burning on the base of the pan.

3 Spoon into clean sterilized jars and seal. When cold, store the jars in the fridge and use within 2 months.

COOK'S TIP
To test the consistency of the finished chutney before bottling, spoon a little of the mixture on to a plate: the chutney is ready once it holds its shape.

Nectarine Relish

This sweet and tangy fruit relish goes very well with hot roast meats and game birds, such as guinea fowl, pheasant and pork. Make while nectarines are plentiful and keep tightly covered in the fridge to serve at Christmas for a really special treat.

MAKES 450G/1LB

INGREDIENTS
  45ml/3 tbsp olive oil
  2 Spanish onions, thinly sliced
  1 fresh green chilli, seeded and finely chopped
  5ml/1 tsp finely chopped fresh rosemary
  2 bay leaves
  450g/1lb nectarines, stoned and cut into chunks
  150g/5oz/1 cup raisins
  10ml/2 tsp crushed coriander seeds
  350g/12oz/2 cups demerara sugar
  200ml/7fl oz/scant 1 cup red wine vinegar

1 Heat the oil in a large pan. Add the onions, chilli, rosemary and bay leaves. Cook, stirring often, for 15–20 minutes or until the onions are soft.

COOK'S TIP
Jars of this relish make a welcome gift. Add a colourful tag reminding the recipient to keep it in the fridge.

2 Add all the remaining ingredients and bring to the boil slowly, stirring often. Lower the heat and simmer for 1 hour or until the relish is thick and sticky, stirring occasionally.

3 Spoon into sterilized jars and seal. Cool, then chill. The relish will keep in the fridge for up to 5 months.

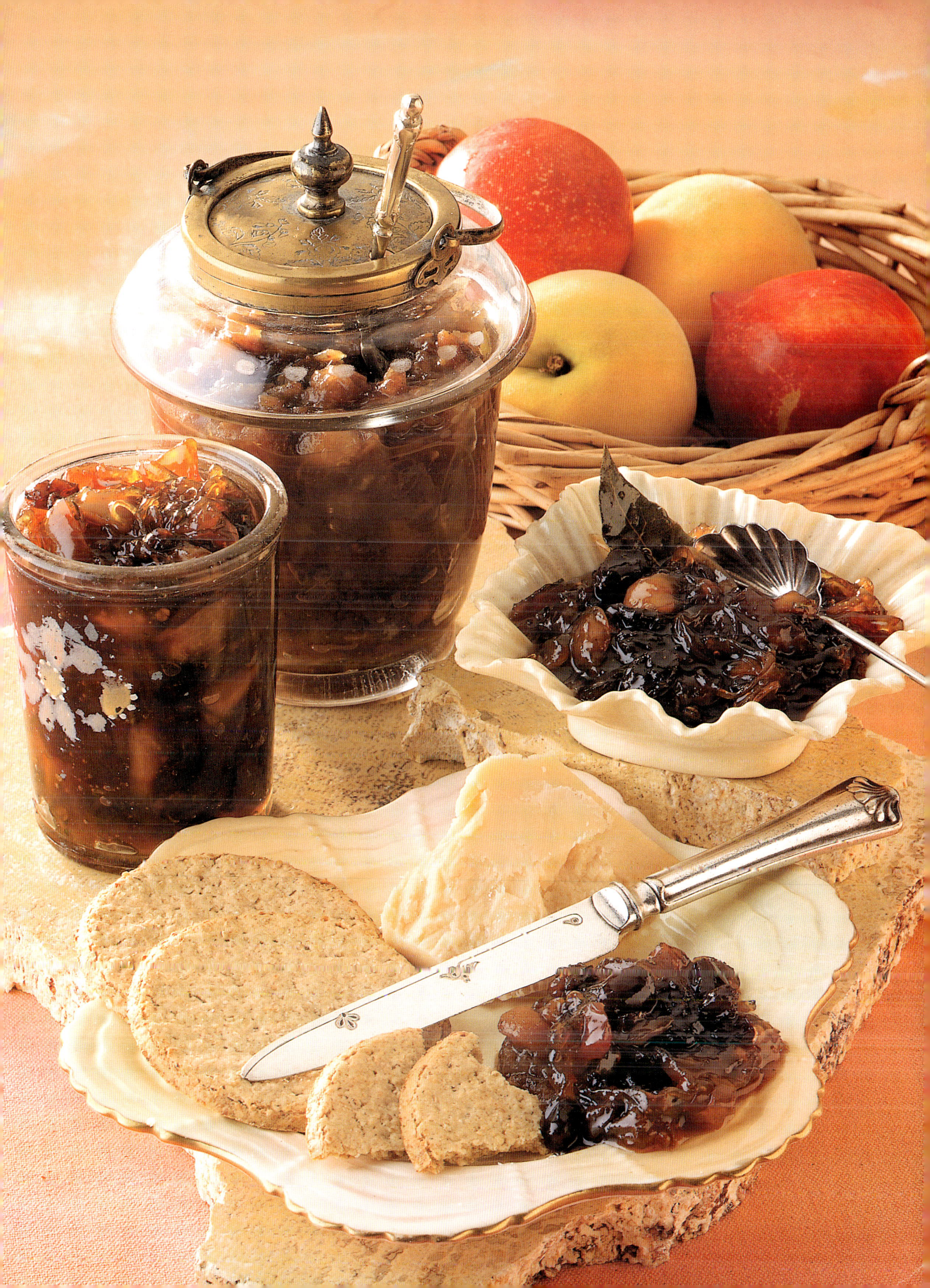

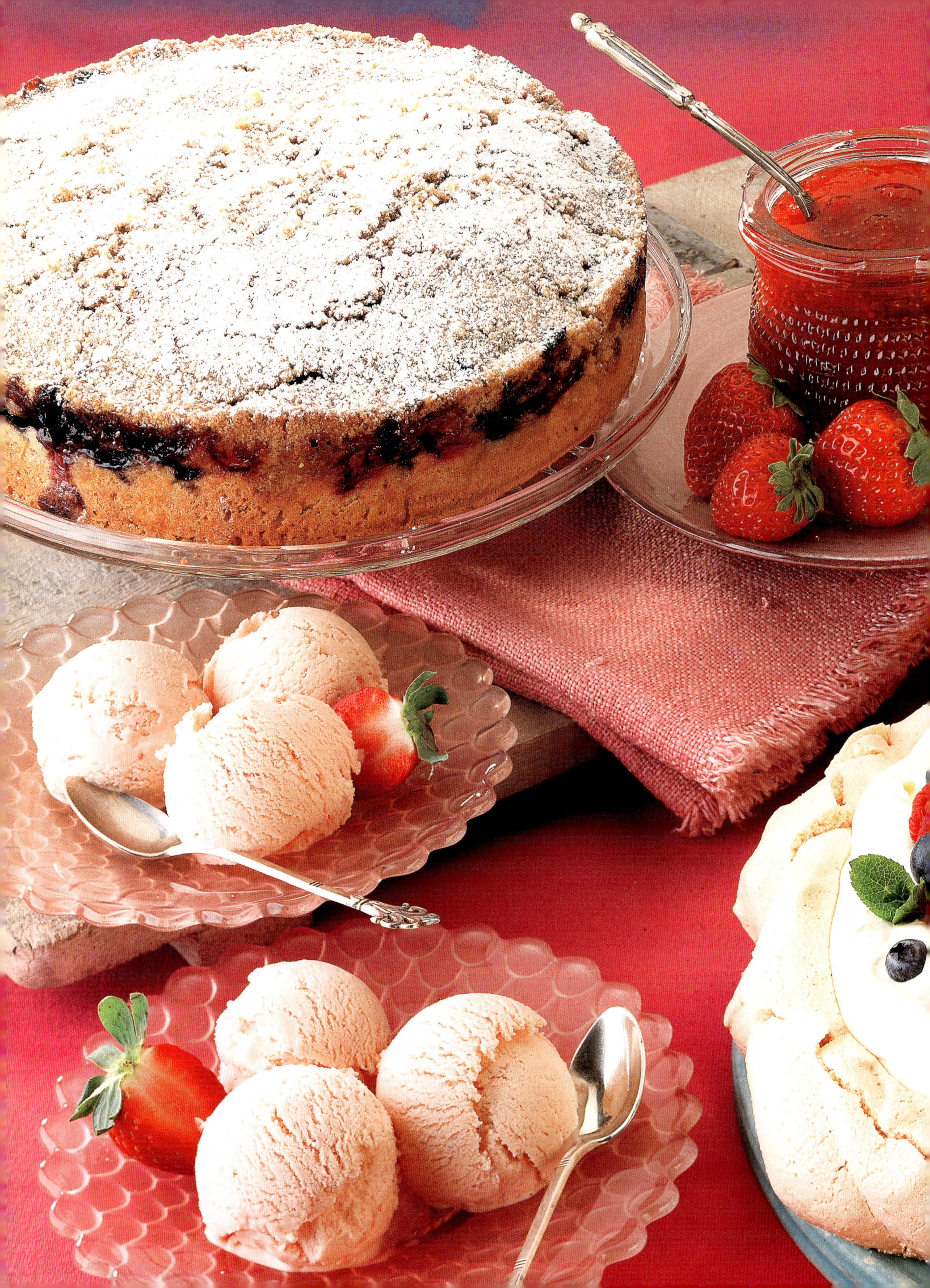

Berry and Currant Recipes

For sheer beauty, berries take a lot of beating. Make the most of their tantalizing colours and flavours by serving them simply, as a topping for shortcakes or in a summer pudding. Fresh Blueberry Muffins, Berry Brûlée Tarts, Bramble Jelly — these are berries at their best.

Summer Pudding

No fruit book would be complete without this well-loved classic recipe. Don't reserve it solely for summer: it freezes well and provides a delicious dessert for Christmas day, as a light and refreshing alternative to the traditional pudding.

SERVES FOUR TO SIX

INGREDIENTS

8 × 1cm/½in thick slices of day-old white bread, crusts removed
800g/1¾lb/6–7 cups mixed berry fruit, such as strawberries, raspberries, blackcurrants, redcurrants and blueberries
50g/2oz/¼ cup golden caster sugar
lightly whipped double cream or crème fraîche, to serve

1 Trim a slice of bread to fit in the base of a 1.2 litre/2 pint/5 cup pudding basin, then trim another 5–6 slices to line the sides of the basin.

2 Place all the fruit in a saucepan with the sugar. Cook gently for 4–5 minutes until the juices begin to run – it will not be necessary to add any water. Allow the mixture to cool slightly, then spoon the berries and enough of their juices to moisten into the bread-lined pudding basin. Save any leftover juice to serve with the pudding.

3 Fold over the excess bread, then cover the fruit with the remaining bread slices, trimming them to fit. Place a small plate or saucer directly on top of the pudding, fitting it inside the basin. Weight it with a 900g/2lb weight if you have one, or use a couple of full cans.

4 Leave the pudding in the fridge for at least 8 hours or overnight. To serve, run a knife between the pudding and the basin and turn it out on to a plate. Spoon any reserved juices over the top and serve with whipped cream or crème fraîche.

Hot Blackberry and Apple Soufflés

As the blackberry season is so short and the apple season so long, it's always worth freezing a bag of blackberries to have on hand for treats like this one.

MAKES SIX

INGREDIENTS
   butter, for greasing
   150g/5oz/⅔ cup caster sugar, plus extra for dusting
   350g/12oz/3 cups blackberries
   1 large cooking apple, peeled, cored and finely diced
   grated rind and juice of 1 orange
   3 egg whites
   icing sugar, for dusting

COOK'S TIP
Running a table knife around the edge of the soufflés before baking helps them to rise evenly without any part sticking to the rim of the dishes.

1 Preheat the oven to 200°C/400°F/Gas 6. Generously grease six 150ml/¼ pint/⅔ cup individual soufflé dishes with butter and dust with caster sugar, shaking out the excess sugar. Put a baking sheet in the oven to heat.

2 Cook the blackberries and diced apple with the orange rind and juice in a pan for 10 minutes or until the apple has pulped down well. Press through a sieve into a bowl. Stir in 50g/2oz/¼ cup of the caster sugar. Set aside to cool.

3 Put a spoonful of the fruit purée into each prepared dish and smooth the surface. Set the dishes aside.

4 Whisk the egg whites in a large grease-free bowl until they form stiff peaks. Very gradually whisk in the remaining caster sugar to make a stiff, glossy meringue mixture.

5 Fold in the remaining fruit purée and spoon the flavoured meringue into the prepared dishes. Level the tops with a palette knife, and run a table knife around the edge of each dish.

6 Place the dishes on the hot baking sheet and bake for 10–15 minutes until the soufflés have risen well and are lightly browned. Dust the tops with icing sugar and serve immediately.

Summer Berry Crêpes

The delicate flavour of these fluffy crêpes contrasts beautifully with tangy berry fruits.

SERVES FOUR

INGREDIENTS
  115g/4oz/1 cup self-raising flour
  1 large egg
  300ml/½ pint/1¼ cups milk
  a few drops of pure vanilla essence
  15g/½oz/1 tbsp butter
  15ml/1 tbsp sunflower oil
  icing sugar, for dusting
For the fruit
  25g/1oz/2 tbsp butter
  50g/2oz/¼ cup caster sugar
  juice of 2 oranges
  thinly pared rind of ½ orange
  350g/12oz/3 cups mixed summer berries, such as sliced strawberries, yellow raspberries, blueberries and redcurrants
  45ml/3 tbsp Grand Marnier or other orange liqueur

1 Preheat the oven to 150°C/300°F/Gas 2. To make the crêpes, sift the flour into a large bowl and make a well in the centre. Break in the egg and gradually whisk in the milk to make a smooth batter. Stir in the vanilla essence. Set the batter aside in a cool place for up to half an hour.

2 Heat the butter and oil together in an 18cm/7in non-stick frying pan. Swirl to grease the pan, then pour off the excess fat into a small bowl.

3 If the batter has been allowed to stand, whisk it thoroughly until smooth. Pour a little of the batter into the hot pan, swirling to cover the base of the pan evenly. Cook until the mixture comes away from the sides and the crêpe is golden underneath.

4 Flip over the crêpe with a large palette knife and cook the other side briefly until golden.

5 Slide the crêpe onto a heatproof plate. Make seven more crêpes in the same way, greasing the pan with more butter and oil mixture as needed. Cover the crêpes with foil or another plate and keep them hot in the oven.

COOK'S TIP
For safety, when igniting a mixture for flambéing, use a long taper or long wooden match. Stand back as you set the mixture alight.

6 To prepare the fruit, melt the butter in a heavy-based frying pan, stir in the sugar and cook gently until the mixture is golden brown. Add the orange juice and rind and cook until syrupy.

7 Add the fruits and warm through, then add the liqueur and set it alight. Shake the pan to incorporate the liqueur until the flame dies down.

8 Fold the pancakes into quarters and arrange two on each plate. Spoon over some of the fruit mixture and dust liberally with the icing sugar. Serve any remaining fruit mixture separately.

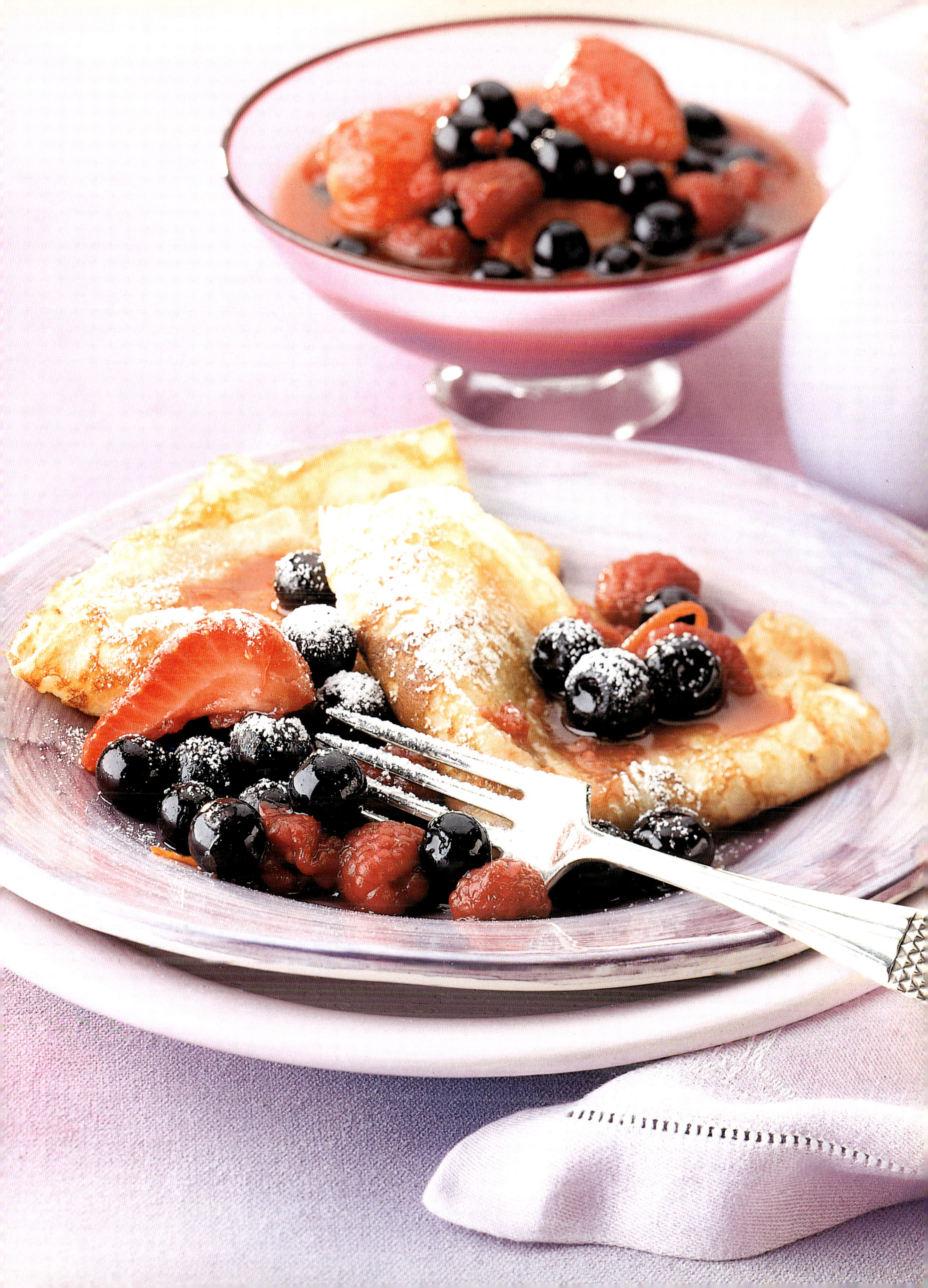

Fresh Berry Pavlova

Pavlova is the simplest of desserts, but it can also be the most stunning. Fill with a mix of berry fruits if you like – raspberries and blueberries make a marvellous combination.

SERVES SIX TO EIGHT

INGREDIENTS
- 4 egg whites, at room temperature
- 225g/8oz/1 cup caster sugar
- 5ml/1 tsp cornflour
- 5ml/1 tsp cider vinegar
- 2.5ml/½ tsp pure vanilla essence
- 300ml/½ pint/1¼ cups double cream
- 150ml/¼ pint/⅔ cup crème fraîche
- 175g/6oz/1 cup raspberries
- 175g/6oz/1½ cups blueberries
- fresh mint sprigs, to decorate
- icing sugar, for dusting

COOK'S TIP
To begin, invert a plate on the baking paper and draw round it with a pencil. Turn the paper over and use the circle as a guide for the meringue.

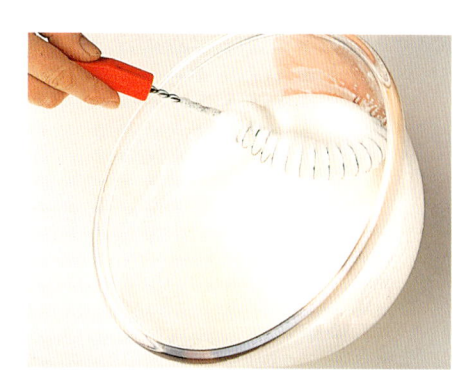

1 Preheat the oven to 140°C/275°F/Gas 1. Line a baking sheet with non-stick baking paper. Whisk the egg whites in a large grease-free bowl until they form stiff peaks. Gradually whisk in the sugar to make a stiff, glossy meringue. Sift the cornflour over and fold it in with the vinegar and vanilla.

2 Spoon the meringue mixture on to the paper-lined sheet, using the circle drawn on the paper as a guide (see Cook's Tip). Spread into a round, swirling the top, and bake for 1¼ hours or until the meringue is crisp and very lightly golden. Switch off the oven, keeping the door closed, and allow the meringue to cool for 1–2 hours.

3 Carefully peel the paper from the meringue and transfer it to a serving plate. Whip the cream in a large mixing bowl until it forms soft peaks, fold in the crème fraîche, then spoon the mixture into the centre of the meringue case. Top with the raspberries and blueberries and decorate with the mint sprigs. Sift icing sugar over the top and serve at once.

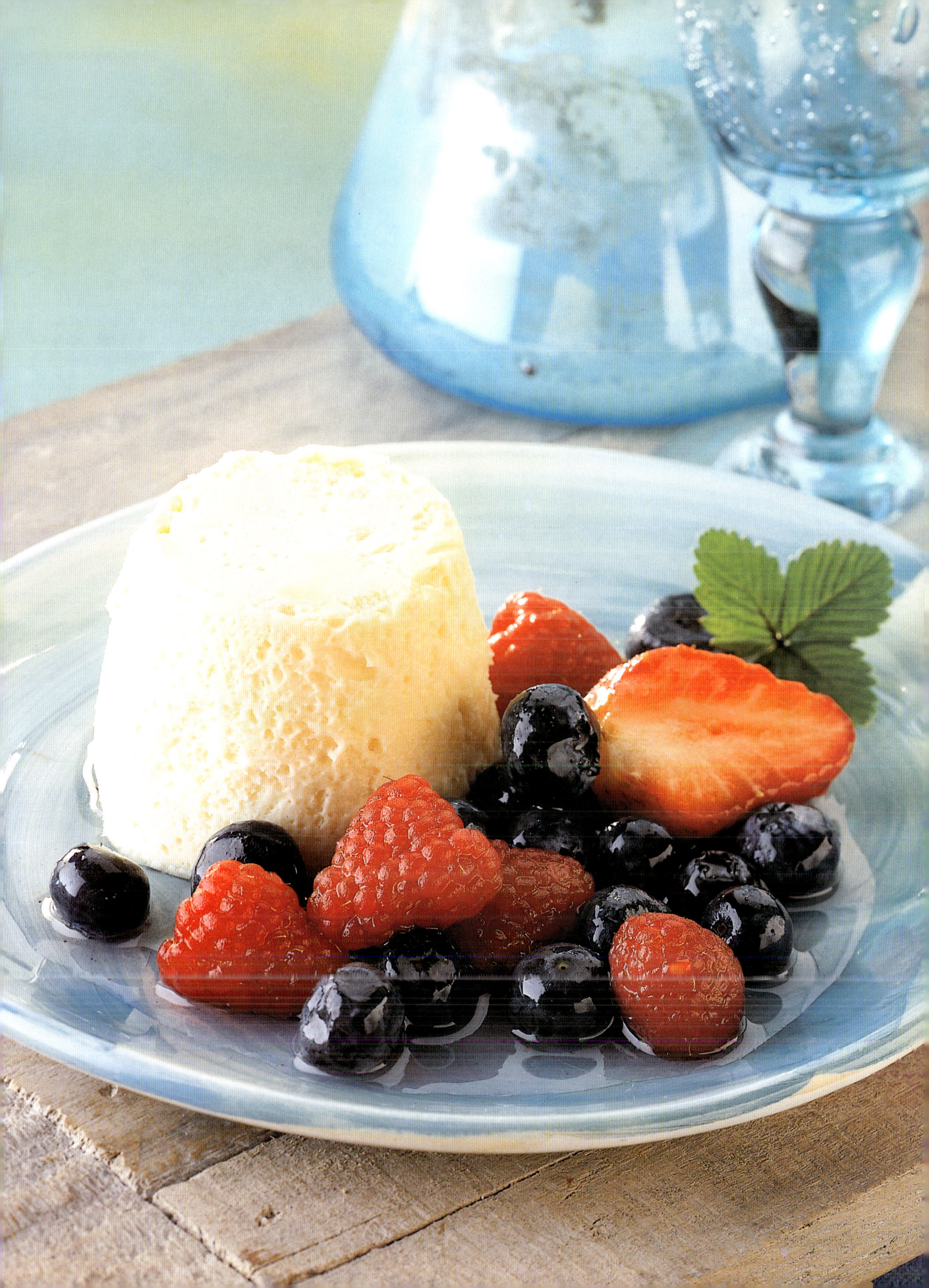

Fresh Strawberry Ice Cream

You can make the ice cream by hand if you freeze it over a period of several hours, whisking it every hour or so, but the texture won't be as good.

SERVES SIX

INGREDIENTS
300ml/½ pint/1¼ cups creamy milk
1 vanilla pod
3 large egg yolks
225g/8oz/1½–2 cups strawberries
juice of ½ lemon
75g/3oz/¾ cup icing sugar
300ml/½ pint/1¼ cups double cream
sliced strawberries, to serve

1 Put the milk into a pan, add the vanilla pod and bring to the boil over a low heat. Remove from the heat. Leave for 20 minutes, then remove the vanilla pod. Strain the warm milk into a bowl containing the egg yolks; whisk well.

2 Return the mixture to the clean pan and heat, stirring, until the custard just coats the back of the spoon. Pour the custard into a bowl, cover the surface with clear film and set aside to cool.

COOK'S TIP
Use free-range eggs if possible, bought from a reputable supplier.

3 Meanwhile, purée the strawberries with the lemon juice in a food processor or blender. Press the strawberry purée through a sieve into a bowl. Stir in the icing sugar and set aside.

4 Whip the cream to soft peaks, then gently but thoroughly fold it into the custard with the strawberry purée. Pour the mixture into an ice cream maker. Churn for 20–30 minutes or until the mixture holds its shape. Transfer the ice cream to a freezerproof container, cover and freeze until firm. Soften briefly before serving with the strawberries.

Blackcurrant Sorbet

THIS LUSCIOUS SORBET IS EASILY MADE BY HAND, BUT IT IS IMPORTANT TO ALTERNATELY FREEZE AND BLEND OR PROCESS THE MIXTURE FIVE OR SIX TIMES TO GET THE BEST RESULT. IF YOU MAKE LOTS OF ICE CREAM AND SORBETS, IT IS WORTH INVESTING IN AN ICE CREAM MAKER.

SERVES SIX

INGREDIENTS
- 300ml/½ pint/1¼ cups water, plus 30ml/2 tbsp
- 115g/4oz/½ cup caster sugar
- 225g/8oz/2 cups blackcurrants
- 30ml/2 tbsp crème de cassis or other blackcurrant liqueur
- 5ml/1 tsp lemon juice
- 2 egg whites

1 Pour 300ml/½ pint/1¼ cups of the water into a saucepan and add the sugar. Place over a low heat until the sugar has dissolved. Bring to the boil and boil rapidly for 10 minutes, then set the syrup aside to cool.

2 Meanwhile, cook the blackcurrants with the remaining 30ml/2 tbsp water over a low heat for 5–7 minutes. Press the blackcurrants and juice through a sieve placed over a jug, then stir the blackcurrant purée into the syrup with the liqueur and lemon juice. Allow to cool completely, then chill for 1 hour.

3 Pour the chilled blackcurrant syrup into a freezerproof bowl; freeze until slushy, whisking occasionally. Whisk the egg whites in a grease-free bowl until they form soft peaks, then fold into the semi-frozen blackcurrant mixture.

4 Freeze the mixture again until firm, then spoon into a food processor or blender and process. Alternately freeze and process or blend until completely smooth. Serve the sorbet straight from the freezer.

56 *Berry and Currant Recipes*

Raspberry and Rose Petal Shortcakes

Rosewater-scented cream and fresh raspberries form the filling for this delectable dessert. Though they look impressive, these shortcakes are easy to make.

MAKES SIX

INGREDIENTS
   115g/4oz/½ cup unsalted
     butter, softened
   50g/2oz/¼ cup caster sugar
   ½ vanilla pod, split, seeds reserved
   115g/4oz/1 cup plain flour, plus
     extra for dusting
   50g/2oz/⅓ cup semolina
   icing sugar, for dusting
For the filling
   300ml/½ pint/1¼ cups double cream
   15ml/1 tbsp icing sugar
   2.5ml/½ tsp rosewater
   450g/1lb/4 cups raspberries
For the decoration
   12 miniature roses, unsprayed
   6 mint sprigs
   1 egg white, beaten
   caster sugar, for dusting

1 Cream the butter, caster sugar and vanilla seeds in a bowl until pale and fluffy. Sift the flour and semolina together, then gradually work the dry ingredients into the creamed mixture to make a biscuit dough.

VARIATIONS
Other soft red summer berries, such as mulberries, loganberries and tayberries, would be equally good in this dessert.

COOK'S TIP
For best results, serve the shortcakes as soon as possible after assembling them. Otherwise, they are likely to turn soggy from the berries' liquid.

2 Gently knead the dough on a lightly floured surface until smooth. Roll out quite thinly and prick all over with a fork. Using a 7.5cm/3in fluted cutter, cut out 12 rounds. Place these on a baking sheet and chill for 30 minutes.

3 Meanwhile, make the filling. Whisk the cream with the icing sugar until soft peaks form. Fold in the rosewater and chill until required.

4 Preheat the oven to 180°C/350°F/Gas 4. To make the decoration, paint the roses and leaves with the egg white. Dust with sugar; dry on a wire rack.

5 Bake the shortcakes for 15 minutes or until lightly golden. Lift them off the baking sheet with a metal fish slice and cool on a wire rack.

6 To assemble the shortcakes, spoon the rosewater cream on to half the biscuits. Add a layer of raspberries, then top with a second shortcake. Dust with icing sugar. Decorate with the frosted roses and mint sprigs.

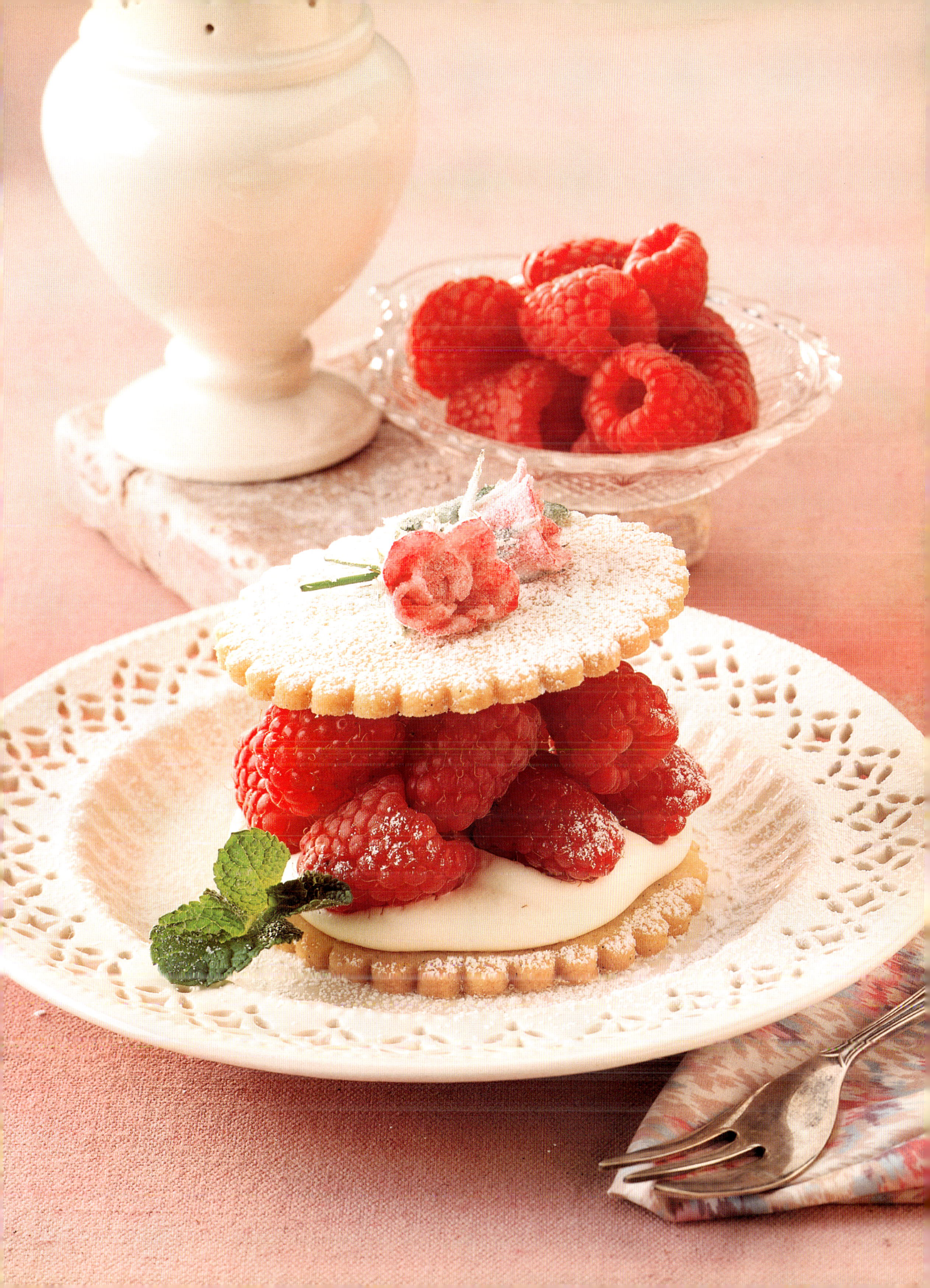

Fresh Currant Bread and Butter Pudding

Fresh mixed currants add a tart touch to this scrumptious hot pudding.

SERVES SIX

INGREDIENTS
8 medium-thick slices day old bread, crusts removed
50g/2oz/¼ cup butter, softened
115g/4oz/1 cup redcurrants
115g/4oz/1 cup blackcurrants
4 eggs, beaten
75g/3oz/6 tbsp caster sugar
475ml/16fl oz/2 cups creamy milk
5ml/1 tsp pure vanilla essence
freshly grated nutmeg
30ml/2 tbsp demerara sugar
single cream, to serve

1 Preheat the oven to 160°C/325°F/Gas 3. Generously butter a 1.2 litre/2 pint/5 cup oval baking dish.

VARIATION
A mixture of blueberries and raspberries would work just as well as the currants.

2 Spread the slices of bread generously with the butter, then cut them in half diagonally. Layer the slices in the dish, buttered side up, scattering the currants between the layers.

3 Beat the eggs and caster sugar lightly together in a large mixing bowl, then gradually whisk in the milk, vanilla essence and a large pinch of freshly grated nutmeg.

4 Pour the milk mixture over the bread, pushing the slices down. Scatter the demerara sugar and a little nutmeg over the top. Place the dish in a baking tin and fill with hot water to come halfway up the sides of the dish. Bake for 40 minutes, then increase the oven temperature to 180°C/350°F/Gas 4 and bake for 20–25 minutes more or until the top is golden. Cool slightly, then serve with single cream.

Cranberry and Blueberry Streusel Cake

Cranberries are seldom used in sweet dishes but once they are sweetened, they have a great flavour and are perfect when partnered with blueberries.

MAKES TEN SLICES

INGREDIENTS
- 175g/6oz/¾ cup butter, softened
- 115g/4oz/½ cup caster sugar
- 350g/12oz/3 cups plain flour
- 2 large eggs, beaten
- 5ml/1 tsp baking powder
- 5ml/1 tsp pure vanilla essence
- 115g/4oz/1 cup cranberries
- 115g/4oz/1 cup blueberries
- 50g/2oz/⅓ cup light muscovado sugar
- 2.5ml/½ tsp crushed cardamom seeds
- icing sugar, for dusting

1 Preheat the oven to 190°C/375°F/Gas 5. Grease and base-line a 21cm/8½in round springform cake tin.

2 Cream the butter and caster sugar together until smooth, then rub in the flour with your fingers until the mixture resembles fine breadcrumbs. Take out 200g/7oz/generous 1 cup of the mixture and set this aside.

3 Beat the eggs, baking powder and vanilla essence into the remaining mixture until soft and creamy. Spoon on to the base of the prepared tin and spread evenly. Arrange the cranberries and blueberries on top, then sprinkle the muscovado sugar over.

4 Stir the cardamom seeds into the reserved flour mixture, then scatter evenly over the top of the fruit. Bake for 50–60 minutes or until the topping is golden. Cool the cake in the tin for 10 minutes, then remove the sides of the tin. Slide it on to a wire rack, lifting it off its base at the same time. Cool the cake completely, then dust with icing sugar and serve with whipped cream.

Fresh Blueberry Muffins

Make these popular American treats in paper cases for moister muffins — if you can't find them, just grease the tin well before filling. These are best served slightly warm.

MAKES TWELVE

INGREDIENTS
 275g/10oz/2½ cups plain flour
 15ml/1 tbsp baking powder
 75g/3oz/6 tbsp caster sugar
 250ml/8fl oz/1 cup milk
 3 eggs, beaten
 115g/4oz/½ cup butter, melted
 a few drops of pure vanilla essence
 225g/8oz/2 cups blueberries
For the topping
 50g/2oz/½ cup pecan nuts,
  coarsely chopped
 30ml/2 tbsp demerara sugar

COOK'S TIP
Don't be tempted to beat the muffin mixture; it should be fairly wet and needs to be quite lumpy. Overmixing will create tough muffins.

1 Preheat the oven to 200°C/400°F/Gas 6. Stand 12 paper muffin cases in a muffin tin, or simply grease the tin thoroughly. Sift the flour and baking powder into a large bowl. Stir in the caster sugar. Mix the milk, eggs, melted butter and vanilla essence in a jug and whisk lightly. Add to the flour mixture and fold together lightly.

2 Fold in the blueberries, then divide the mixture among the muffin cases. Scatter a few nuts and a little demerara sugar over the top of each. Bake for 20–25 minutes, or until the muffins are well risen and golden.

3 Remove the warm muffins from the tin; cool slightly on a wire rack.

Berry and Currant Recipes 61

BLUEBERRY PIE

AMERICAN BLUEBERRIES OR EUROPEAN BILBERRIES CAN BE USED FOR THIS PIE. YOU MAY NEED TO ADD A LITTLE MORE SUGAR IF YOU ARE LUCKY ENOUGH TO FIND NATIVE BILBERRIES.

SERVES SIX

INGREDIENTS
- 2 × 225g/8oz ready-rolled shortcrust pastry sheets, thawed if frozen
- 800g/1¾lb/7 cups blueberries
- 75g/3oz/6 tbsp caster sugar, plus extra for sprinkling
- 45ml/3 tbsp cornflour
- grated rind and juice of ½ orange
- grated rind of ½ lemon
- 2.5ml/½ tsp ground cinnamon
- 15g/½oz/1 tbsp unsalted butter, diced
- beaten egg, to glaze
- whipped cream, to serve

1 Preheat the oven to 200°C/400°F/Gas 6. Use one sheet of pastry to line a 23cm/9in pie tin, leaving the excess pastry hanging over the edges.

2 Mix the blueberries, caster sugar, cornflour, orange rind and juice, lemon rind and cinnamon in a large bowl. Spoon into the pastry case and dot with the butter. Dampen the rim of the pastry case with a little water and top with the remaining pastry sheet.

VARIATION
Substitute a crumble topping for the pastry lid. The contrast with the juicy blueberry filling is sensational.

3 Cut the pastry edge at 2.5cm/1in intervals, then fold each section over on itself to form a triangle and create a sunflower edge. Trim off the excess pastry and cut out decorations from the trimmings. Attach them to the pastry lid with a little of the beaten egg.

4 Glaze the pastry with the egg and sprinkle with caster sugar. Bake for 30–35 minutes or until golden. Serve warm or cold with whipped cream.

Berry Brûlée Tarts

THIS QUANTITY OF PASTRY IS ENOUGH FOR EIGHT TARTLETS, SO FREEZE HALF FOR ANOTHER DAY. THE BRÛLÉE TOPPING IS BEST ADDED NO MORE THAN TWO HOURS BEFORE SERVING THE TARTS.

MAKES FOUR

INGREDIENTS
- 250g/9oz/2¼ cups plain flour
- pinch of salt
- 25g/1oz/¼ cup ground almonds
- 15ml/1 tbsp icing sugar
- 150g/5oz/⅔ cup unsalted butter, chilled and diced
- 1 egg yolk
- about 45ml/3 tbsp cold water

For the filling
- 4 egg yolks
- 15ml/1 tbsp cornflour
- 50g/2oz/¼ cup caster sugar
- a few drops of pure vanilla essence
- 300ml/½ pint/1¼ cups creamy milk
- 225g/8oz/2 cups mixed berry fruits, such as small strawberries, raspberries, blackcurrants and redcurrants
- 50g/2oz/½ cup icing sugar

1 Mix the flour, salt, ground almonds and icing sugar in a bowl. Rub in the butter by hand or in a food processor until the mixture resembles fine breadcrumbs. Add the egg yolk and enough cold water to form a dough. Knead the dough gently, then cut it in half and freeze half for use later.

2 Cut the remaining pastry into four equal pieces and roll out thinly.

COOK'S TIP
If you possess a culinary blow torch – and are confident about operating it safely – use it to easily melt and caramelize the brûlée topping.

3 Use the pastry rounds to line four individual tartlet tins, letting the excess pastry hang over the edges. Chill for 30 minutes.

4 Preheat the oven to 200°C/400°F/Gas 6. Line the pastry with non-stick baking paper and baking beans. Bake blind for 10 minutes. Remove the paper and beans and return the tartlet cases to the oven for 5 minutes until golden. Allow the pastry to cool, then carefully trim off the excess pastry.

5 Beat the egg yolks, cornflour, caster sugar and vanilla essence in a bowl.

6 Warm the milk in a heavy-based pan, pour it on to the egg yolks, whisking constantly, then return the mixture to the clean pan.

7 Heat, stirring, until the custard thickens, but do not let it boil. Remove from the heat, press a piece of clear film directly on the surface of the custard and allow to cool.

8 Scatter the berries in the tartlet cases and spoon over the custard. Chill the tarts for 2 hours.

9 To serve, sift icing sugar generously over the tops of the tartlets. Preheat the grill to the highest setting. Place the tartlets under the hot grill until the sugar melts and caramelizes. Allow the topping to cool and harden for about 10 minutes before serving the tarts.

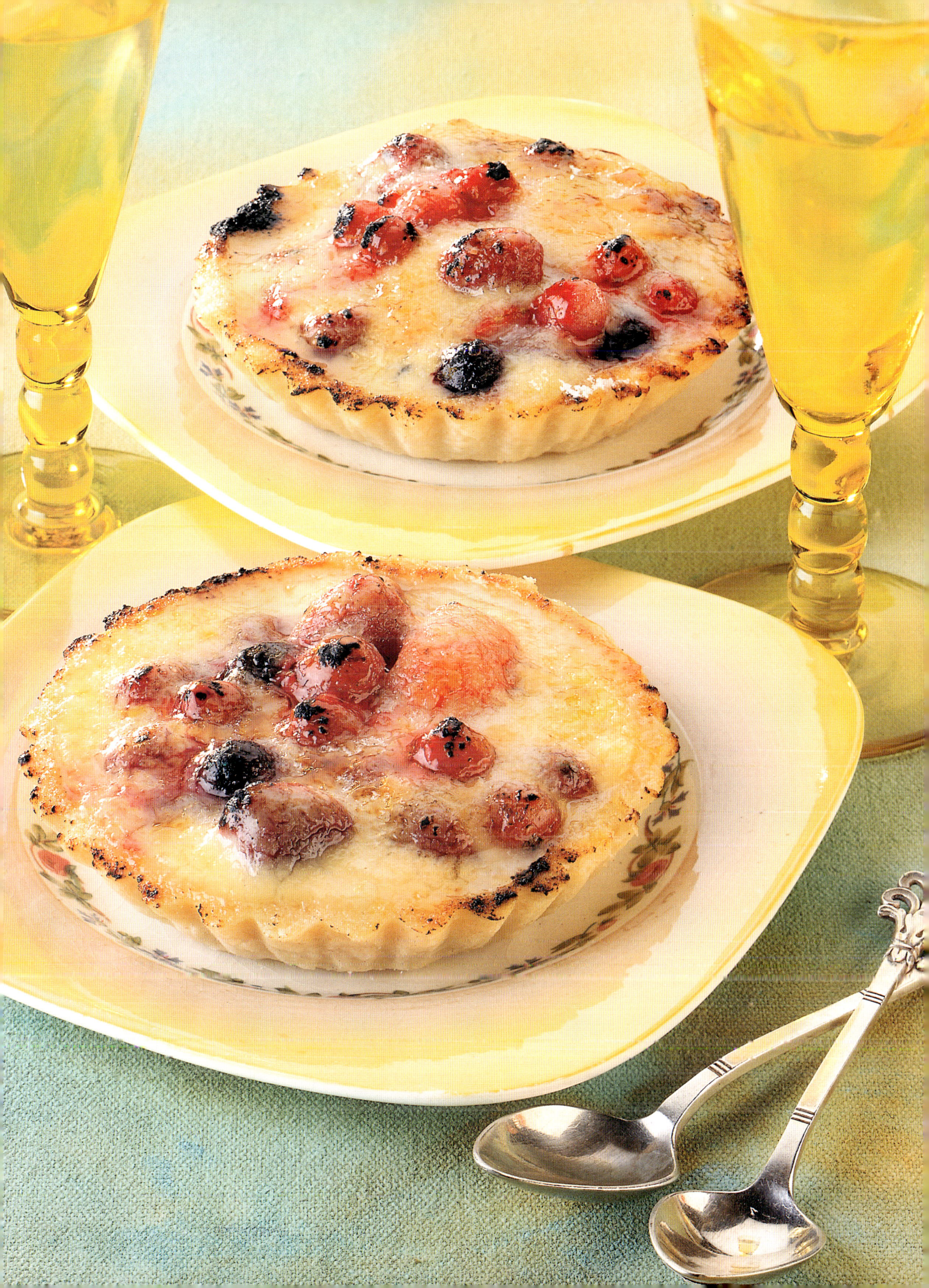

BRAMBLE JELLY

This jelly is one of the best. It has to be made with hand-picked wild blackberries for the best flavour. Make sure you include a few red unripe berries for a good set.

MAKES 900G/2LB

INGREDIENTS
900g/2lb/8 cups blackberries
300ml/½ pint/1¼ cups water
juice of 1 lemon
about 900g/2lb/4 cups caster sugar
hot buttered toast or English muffins, to serve

VARIATION
Redcurrant jelly is made in the same way, but with less sugar. Reduce the quantity to 350g/12oz/1½ cups for every 600ml/1 pint/2½ cups juice.

1 Put the fruit, water and lemon juice into a large saucepan. Cover the pan and cook for 15–30 minutes or until the blackberries are very soft.

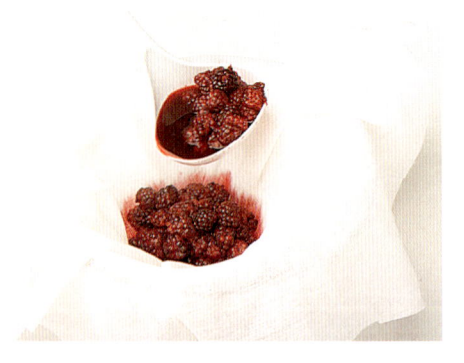

2 Ladle into a jelly bag or a large sieve lined with muslin and set over a large bowl. Leave to drip overnight to obtain the maximum amount of juice.

3 Discard the fruit pulp. Measure the exuded juice and allow 450g/1lb/2 cups sugar to every 600ml/1 pint/2½ cups juice. Place both in a large heavy-based pan and bring the mixture slowly to a boil, stirring all the time until the sugar has dissolved.

4 Boil rapidly until the jelly registers 105°C/220°F on a sugar thermometer or test for setting by spooning a small amount on to a chilled saucer. Chill for 3 minutes, then push the mixture with your finger; if wrinkles form on the surface, it is ready. Cool for 10 minutes.

5 Skim off any scum and pour the jelly into warm sterilized jars. Cover and seal while the jelly is still hot and label when the jars are cold. Serve the jelly with hot buttered toast or English muffins.

Strawberry Jam

Capture the essence of summer in a jar of home-made strawberry jam.

MAKES ABOUT 1.4KG/3LB

INGREDIENTS

1kg/2¼lb/8 cups small strawberries
900g/2lb/4 cups granulated sugar
juice of 2 lemons
scones and clotted cream, to serve

1 Layer the strawberries and sugar in a large bowl. Cover and leave overnight.

2 The next day, scrape the strawberries and their juice into a large heavy-based pan. Add the lemon juice. Gradually bring to the boil over a low heat, stirring until the sugar has dissolved.

COOK'S TIPS

For best results when making jam, don't wash the strawberries unless absolutely necessary. Instead, brush off any dirt, or wipe the strawberries with a damp cloth. If you have to wash any, pat them dry and then spread them out on a clean dish towel to dry further.

To sterilize jam jars, wash in hot soapy water, then rinse thoroughly and drain. Place the jars on a baking sheet and dry in a warm oven for 15–20 minutes.

3 Boil steadily for 10–15 minutes or until the jam registers 105°C/220°F on a sugar thermometer. Alternatively, test for setting by spooning a small amount on to a chilled saucer. Chill for 3 minutes, then push the jam with your finger; if wrinkles form on the surface, it is ready. Cool for 10 minutes.

4 Pour the strawberry jam into warm sterilized jars, filling them right to the top. Cover and seal while the jam is still hot and label when the jars are cold. Serve with scones and clotted cream, if you like. This jam can be stored in a cool dark place and should keep for up to 1 year.

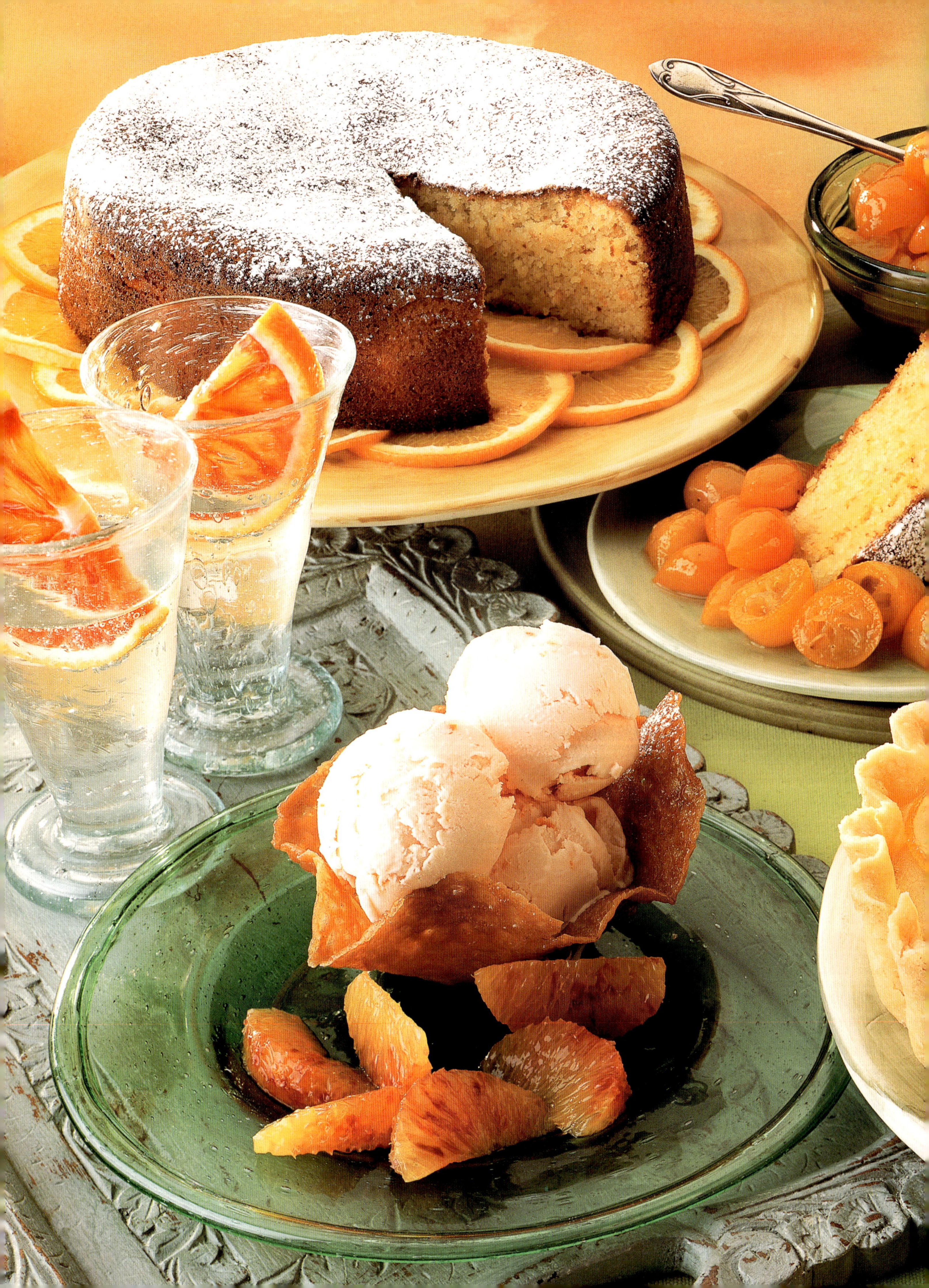

Citrus Fruit Recipes

Put the squeeze on citrus for some of the finest puddings and preserves in the good cook's repertoire. Lemon Surprise Pudding, Moist Orange and Almond Cake, Key Lime Pie and Lemon Meringue Pie are perennially popular, while new delights include Lemon Coeur à la Crème with Cointreau Oranges.

Lemon Coeur À La Crème with Cointreau Oranges

This zesty dessert is the ideal choice to follow a rich main course such as roast pork.

SERVES FOUR

INGREDIENTS
- 225g/8oz/1 cup cottage cheese
- 250g/9oz/generous 1 cup mascarpone cheese
- 50g/2oz/¼ cup caster sugar
- grated rind and juice of 1 lemon
- spirals of orange rind, to decorate

For the Cointreau oranges
- 4 oranges
- 10ml/2 tsp cornflour
- 15ml/1 tbsp icing sugar
- 60ml/4 tbsp Cointreau

1 Put the cottage cheese in a food processor or blender and whizz until smooth. Add the mascarpone, caster sugar, lemon rind and juice and process briefly to mix the ingredients.

2 Line four coeur à la crème moulds with muslin, then divide the mixture among them. Level the surface of each, then place the moulds on a plate to catch any liquid that drains from the cheese. Cover and chill overnight.

3 Make the Cointreau oranges. Squeeze the juice from two oranges and pour into a measuring jug. Make the juice up to 250ml/8fl oz/1 cup with water, then pour into a small saucepan. Blend a little of the juice mixture with the cornflour and add to the pan with the icing sugar. Heat the sauce, stirring until thickened.

4 Using a sharp knife, peel and segment the remaining oranges. Add the segments to the pan, stir to coat, then set aside. When cool, stir in the Cointreau. Cover and chill overnight.

5 Turn the moulds out on to plates and surround with the oranges. Decorate with spirals of orange rind and serve at once.

Clementine Jelly

Jelly isn't only for children: this adult version has a clear fruity taste and can be made extra special by adding a little white rum or Cointreau.

SERVES FOUR

INGREDIENTS
 12 clementines
 clear grape juice (see method for amount)
 15ml/1 tbsp powdered gelatine
 30ml/2 tbsp caster sugar
 whipped cream, to decorate

VARIATION
Use four ruby grapefruit instead of clementines, if you prefer. Squeeze the juice from half of them and segment the rest, discarding any bitter white pith.

1 Squeeze the juice from eight of the clementines and pour it into a jug. Make up to 600ml/1 pint/2½ cups with the grape juice, then strain the juice mixture through a fine sieve.

2 Pour half the juice mixture into a pan. Sprinkle the gelatine on top, leave for 5 minutes, then heat gently until the gelatine has dissolved. Stir in the sugar, then the remaining juice; set aside.

3 Pare the rind very thinly from the remaining fruit and set it aside. Using a small sharp knife, cut between the membrane and fruit to separate the citrus segments. Discard the membrane and white pith.

4 Place half the segments in four dessert glasses and cover with some of the liquid fruit jelly. Place in the fridge and allow to set.

5 When the jellies are set, arrange the remaining segments on top. Carefully pour over the remaining liquid jelly and chill until set. Cut the pared clementine rind into fine shreds. Serve the jellies topped with a generous spoonful of whipped cream scattered with clementine rind shreds.

Ruby Orange Sherbet in Ginger Baskets

THIS SUPERB FROZEN DESSERT IS PERFECT FOR PEOPLE WITHOUT ICE CREAM MAKERS WHO CAN'T BE BOTHERED WITH THE FREEZING AND STIRRING THAT HOME-MADE ICES NORMALLY REQUIRE. IT IS ALSO IDEAL FOR SERVING AT A SPECIAL DINNER PARTY AS BOTH THE SHERBET AND GINGER BASKETS CAN BE MADE IN ADVANCE AND THE DESSERT SIMPLY ASSEMBLED BETWEEN COURSES.

SERVES SIX

INGREDIENTS
- grated rind and juice of 2 blood oranges
- 175g/6oz/1½ cups icing sugar
- 300ml/½ pint/1¼ cups double cream
- 200g/7oz/scant 1 cup Greek-style natural yogurt
- blood orange segments, to decorate (optional)

For the ginger baskets
- 25g/1oz/2 tbsp unsalted butter
- 15ml/1 tbsp golden syrup
- 30ml/2 tbsp caster sugar
- 1.5ml/¼ tsp ground ginger
- 15ml/1 tbsp finely chopped mixed citrus peel
- 15ml/1 tbsp plain flour

1 Place the orange rind and juice in a bowl. Sift the icing sugar over the top and set aside for 30 minutes, then stir until smooth.

2 Whisk the double cream in a large bowl until the mixture forms soft peaks, then fold in the yogurt.

3 Gently stir in the orange juice mixture, then pour into a freezerproof container. Cover and freeze until firm.

4 Make the baskets. Preheat the oven to 180°C/350°F/Gas 4. Place the butter, syrup and sugar in a heavy-based saucepan and heat gently until melted.

5 Add the ground ginger, mixed citrus peel and flour and stir until the mixture is smooth.

6 Lightly grease two baking sheets. Using about 10ml/2 tsp of the mixture at a time, drop three portions of the ginger dough on to each baking sheet, spacing them well apart. Spread each one to a 5cm/2in circle, then bake for 12–14 minutes or until the biscuits are dark golden in colour.

7 Remove the biscuits from the oven and allow to stand on the baking sheets for 1 minute to firm slightly. Lift off with a fish slice and drape over six greased mini pudding tins or upturned cups; flatten the top (which will become the base) and flute the edges to form a basket shape.

8 When cool, lift the baskets off the tins or cups and place on individual dessert plates. Arrange small scoops of the frozen orange sherbet in each basket. Decorate each portion with a few orange segments, if you like.

COOK'S TIP
When making the ginger baskets it is essential to work quickly. Have the greased tins or cups ready before you start. If the biscuits cool and firm up before you have time to drape them all, return them to the oven for a few seconds to soften them again.

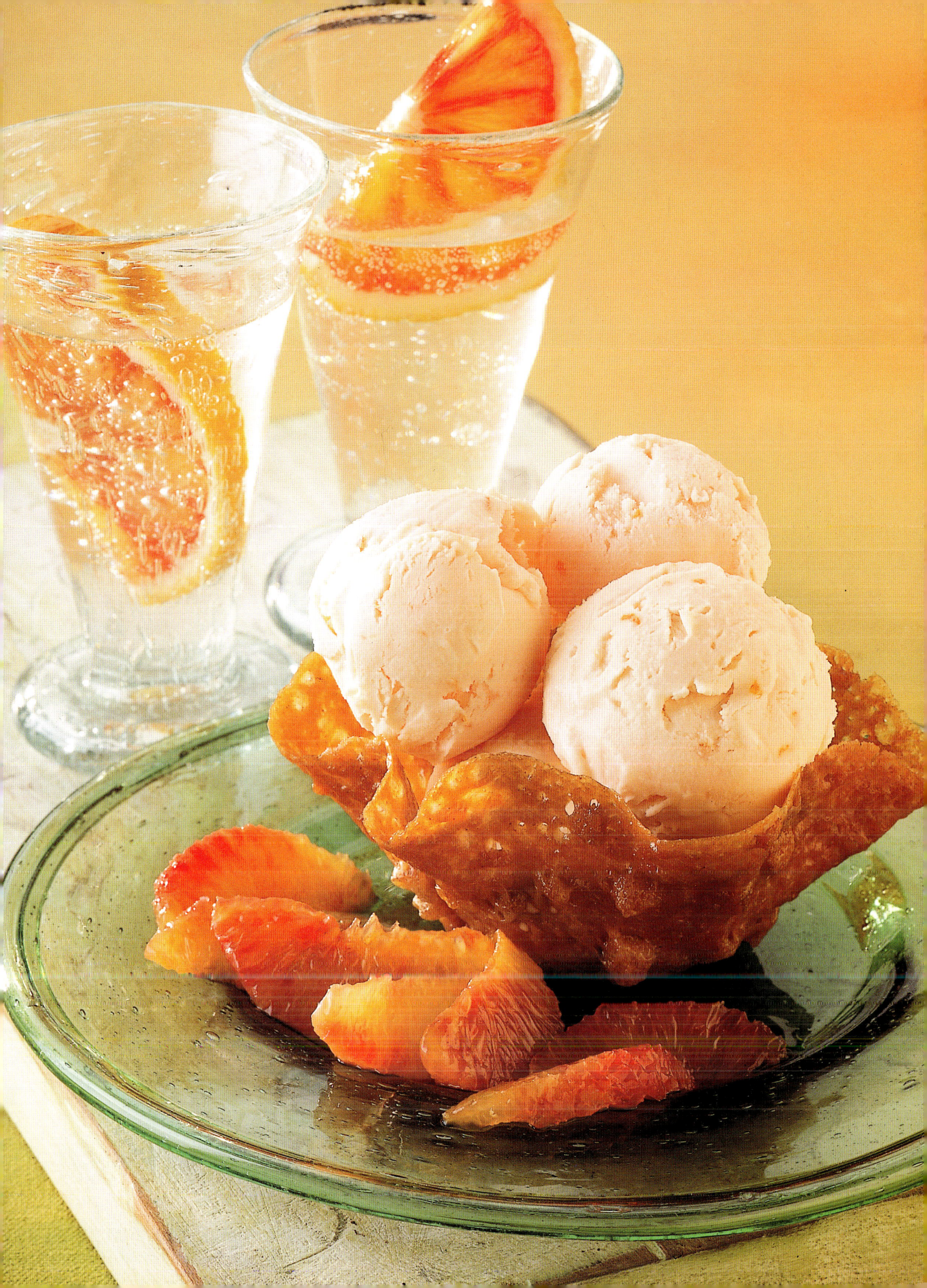

Chocolate and Mandarin Truffle Slice

Chocoholics will love this wickedly rich dessert. The mandarins give it a delicious tang.

SERVES EIGHT

INGREDIENTS
  400g/14oz plain chocolate
  4 egg yolks
  3 mandarin oranges
  200ml/7fl oz/scant 1 cup crème fraîche
  30ml/2 tbsp raisins
  chocolate curls, to decorate
For the sauce
  30ml/2 tbsp Cointreau
  120ml/4fl oz/½ cup crème fraîche

1 Grease a 450g/1lb loaf tin and line it with clear film. Break the chocolate in to a large heatproof bowl. Place over a pan of hot water until melted.

2 Remove the bowl of chocolate from the heat and whisk in the egg yolks.

COOK'S TIP
Chocolate-tipped mandarin slices would also make a superb decoration. Use small segments; pat dry on kitchen paper, then half dip them in melted chocolate. Leave on non-stick baking paper until the chocolate has set.

3 Pare the rind from the mandarins, taking care to leave the pith behind. Cut the rind into slivers.

4 Stir the slivers of mandarin rind into the chocolate with the crème fraîche and raisins. Beat until smooth, then spoon the mixture into the prepared loaf tin and chill for 4 hours.

5 Cut the pith and any remaining rind from the mandarins, then slice thinly.

6 For the sauce, stir the Cointreau into the crème fraîche. Remove the truffle loaf from the tin, peel off the clear film and slice. Serve each slice on a dessert plate with some sauce and mandarin slices, and decorate.

Citrus Fruit Recipes 73

Lemon and Lime Cheesecake

TANGY LEMON CHEESECAKES ARE ALWAYS A HIT. THE LIME SYRUP MAKES THIS A CITRUS SENSATION.

2 Make the topping. Place the lemon rind and juice in a small saucepan and sprinkle over the gelatine. Leave to sponge for 5 minutes. Heat gently until the gelatine has melted, then set the mixture aside to cool slightly. Beat the ricotta cheese and sugar in a bowl. Stir in the cream and egg yolks, then whisk in the cooled gelatine mixture.

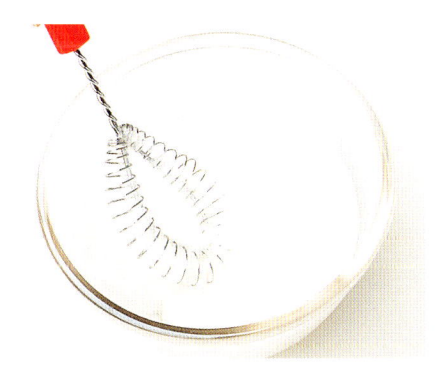

MAKES EIGHT SLICES

INGREDIENTS
   150g/5oz/1½ cups digestive biscuits
   40g/1½oz/3 tbsp butter
For the topping
   grated rind and juice of 2 lemons
   10ml/2 tsp powdered gelatine
   250g/9oz/generous 1 cup ricotta
      cheese
   75g/3oz/⅓ cup caster sugar
   150ml/¼ pint/⅔ cup double cream
   2 eggs, separated
For the lime syrup
   finely pared rind and juice of 3 limes
   75g/3oz/⅓ cup caster sugar
   5ml/1 tsp arrowroot mixed with
      30ml/2 tbsp water
   a little green food colouring
      (optional)

1 Lightly grease a 20cm/8in round springform cake tin. Place the biscuits in a food processor or blender and process until they form fine crumbs. Melt the butter in a large saucepan, then stir in the crumbs until well coated. Spoon into the prepared cake tin, press the crumbs down well in an even layer, then chill.

3 Whisk the egg whites in a grease-free bowl until they form soft peaks. Fold them into the cheese mixture. Spoon on to the biscuit base, level the surface and chill for 2–3 hours.

4 Meanwhile, make the lime syrup. Place the lime rind, juice and caster sugar in a small saucepan. Bring to the boil, stirring, then boil the syrup for 5 minutes. Stir in the arrowroot mixture and continue to stir until the syrup boils again and thickens slightly. Tint pale green with a little food colouring, if you like. Cool, then chill until required.

5 Spoon the lime syrup over the set cheesecake. Remove from the tin and cut into slices to serve.

74   Citrus Fruit Recipes

Lemon Surprise Pudding

THIS IS A MUCH-LOVED DESSERT MANY OF US REMEMBER FROM CHILDHOOD. THE SURPRISE IS THE UNEXPECTED SAUCE CONCEALED BENEATH THE DELECTABLE SPONGE.

SERVES FOUR

INGREDIENTS
 50g/2oz/¼ cup butter, plus extra
   for greasing
 grated rind and juice of 2 lemons
 115g/4oz/½ cup caster sugar
 2 eggs, separated
 50g/2oz/½ cup self-raising flour
 300ml/½ pint/1¼ cups milk

1 Preheat the oven to 190°C/375°F/Gas 5. Use a little butter to grease a 1.2 litre/2 pint/5 cup baking dish.

2 Beat the lemon rind, remaining butter and caster sugar in a bowl until pale and fluffy. Add the egg yolks and flour and beat together well. Gradually whisk in the lemon juice and milk (don't be alarmed if the mixture curdles horribly!). In a grease-free bowl whisk the egg whites until they form stiff peaks.

3 Fold the egg whites lightly into the lemon mixture, then pour into the prepared baking dish.

4 Place the dish in a roasting tin and pour in hot water to come halfway up the side of the dish. Bake for about 45 minutes until golden. Serve at once.

Crêpes Suzette

SIMPLY SUPERB — THAT'S THE VERDICT ON THIS PERENNIALLY POPULAR DESSERT. THESE CRÊPES DESERVE NOTHING LESS THAN THE BEST QUALITY VANILLA ICE CREAM YOU CAN FIND.

SERVES FOUR

INGREDIENTS
 8 crêpes (see Summer Berry Crêpes
   for method)
 25g/1oz/2 tbsp unsalted butter
 50g/2oz/¼ cup caster sugar
 juice of 2 oranges
 juice of ½ lemon
 60ml/4 tbsp Cointreau or other
   orange liqueur
 best quality vanilla ice cream,
   to serve

COOK'S TIP
Crêpes freeze well and can be reheated by the method described in step 1, or simultaneously thawed and reheated in the microwave. A stack of eight crêpes, interleaved with greaseproof paper, will take 2–3 minutes on High (100% power). Be sure to cover the top crêpe with paper as well.

1 Warm the cooked crêpes between two plates placed over a saucepan of simmering water.

2 Melt the butter in a heavy-based frying pan. Stir in the caster sugar and cook over a medium heat, tilting the pan occasionally, until the mixture is golden brown. Add the orange and lemon juices and stir until the caramel has completely dissolved.

3 Add a crêpe to the pan. Using kitchen tongs, fold it in half, then in half again. Slide to the side of the pan. Repeat with the remaining crêpes.

4 When all the crêpes have been folded in the sauce, pour over the Cointreau and set it alight. Shake the pan until the flames die down. Divide the crêpes and sauce among dessert plates and serve at once with vanilla ice cream.

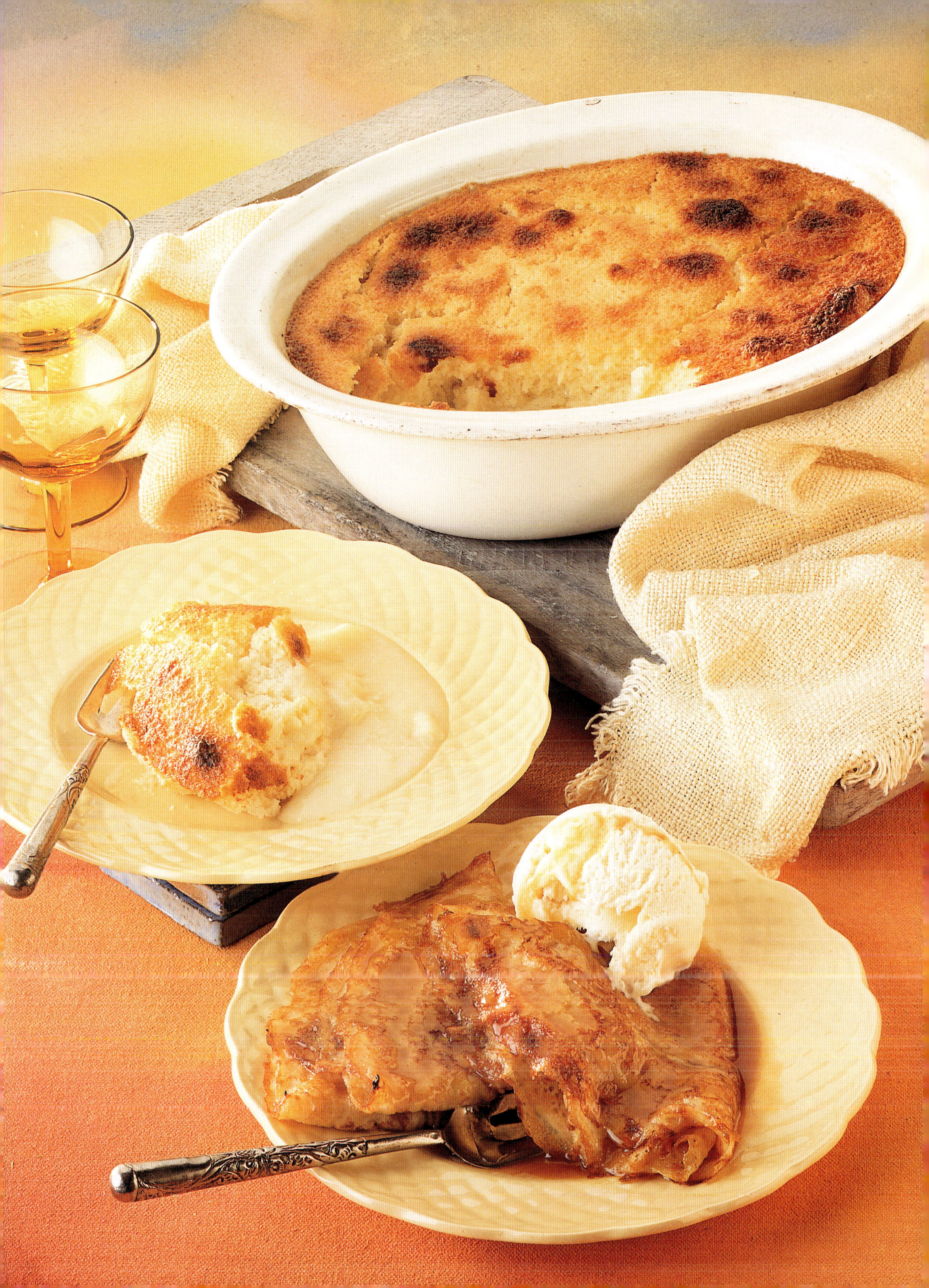

Citrus Fruit Flambé with Pistachio Praline

A fruit flambé makes a dramatic finale for a dinner party. Topping this refreshing citrus fruit dessert with crunchy pistachio praline makes it extra special.

SERVES FOUR

INGREDIENTS
 4 oranges
 2 ruby grapefruit
 2 limes
 50g/2oz/¼ cup butter
 50g/2oz/⅓ cup light muscovado sugar
 45ml/3 tbsp Cointreau
 fresh mint sprigs, to decorate
For the praline
 oil, for greasing
 115g/4oz/½ cup caster sugar
 50g/2oz/½ cup pistachio nuts

1 First, make the pistachio praline. Brush a baking sheet lightly with oil. Place the caster sugar and nuts in a small heavy-based saucepan and cook gently, swirling the pan occasionally until the sugar has melted.

2 Continue to cook over a fairly low heat until the nuts start to pop and the sugar has turned a dark golden colour. Pour on to the oiled baking sheet and set aside to cool. Using a sharp knife, chop the praline into rough chunks.

3 Cut off all the rind and pith from the citrus fruit. Holding each fruit in turn over a large bowl, cut between the membranes so that the segments fall into the bowl, with any juice.

COOK'S TIP
If desired, use a rolling pin or toffee hammer to break up the praline.

4 Heat the butter and muscovado sugar together in a heavy-based frying pan until the sugar has melted and the mixture is golden. Strain the citrus juices into the pan and continue to cook, stirring occasionally, until the juice has reduced and is syrupy.

5 Add the fruit segments and warm through without stirring. Pour over the Cointreau and set it alight. As soon as the flames die down, spoon the fruit flambé into serving dishes. Scatter some praline over each portion and decorate with mint. Serve at once.

Cold Lemon Soufflé with Caramelized Almond Topping

This terrific-to-look-at, refreshing dessert soufflé is light and luscious.

SERVES SIX

INGREDIENTS
 oil, for greasing
 grated rind and juice of
  3 large lemons
 5 large eggs, separated
 115g/4oz/½ cup caster sugar
 25ml/1½ tbsp powdered gelatine
 450ml/¾ pint/scant 2 cups double
  cream
For the decoration
 75g/3oz/¾ cup flaked almonds
 75g/3oz/¾ cup icing sugar
 3 physalis

COOK'S TIP
When peeling off the soufflé collar, hold the blade of a knife against the set soufflé so that it keeps its shape.

1 Make the soufflé collar. Cut a strip of non-stick baking paper long enough to fit around a 900ml/1½ pint/3¾ cup soufflé dish and wide enough to extend 7.5cm/3in above the rim. Fit the strip around the dish, tape, then tie it around the top of the dish with string. Brush the inside of the paper lightly with oil.

2 Put the lemon rind and egg yolks in a bowl. Add 75g/3oz/6 tbsp of the caster sugar and whisk until light and creamy.

3 Place the lemon juice in a small heatproof bowl and sprinkle over the gelatine. Set aside for 5 minutes, then place the bowl in a pan of simmering water. Heat, stirring occasionally, until the gelatine has dissolved. Cool slightly, then stir the gelatine mixture into the egg yolk mixture.

4 In a separate bowl, lightly whip the cream to soft peaks. Fold into the egg yolk mixture and set aside.

5 Whisk the egg whites in a grease-free bowl until stiff peaks form. Gradually whisk in the remaining caster sugar until the mixture is stiff and glossy. Quickly and lightly fold the whites into the yolk mixture. Pour into the prepared dish, smooth the surface and chill for 4–5 hours or until set.

6 Make the decoration. Brush a baking sheet lightly with oil. Preheat the grill. Scatter the almonds over the sheet and sift the icing sugar over. Grill until the nuts are golden and the sugar has caramelized. Allow to cool, then remove the mixture from the tray with a palette knife and break it into pieces.

7 When the soufflé has set, carefully peel off the paper. Pile the caramelized almonds on top of the soufflé and decorate with the physalis.

Lemon Roulade with Lemon Curd Cream

This featherlight roulade filled with a rich lemon curd cream makes a marvellous dessert or tea-time treat. The lemon curd can be made ahead and kept in the fridge.

MAKES EIGHT SLICES

INGREDIENTS
- 4 eggs, separated
- 115g/4oz/½ cup caster sugar
- finely grated rind of 2 lemons
- 5ml/1 tsp pure vanilla essence
- 25g/1oz/¼ cup ground almonds
- 40g/1½oz/⅓ cup plain flour, sifted
- 45ml/3 tbsp icing sugar, for dusting

For the lemon curd cream
- 300ml/½ pint/1¼ cups double cream
- 60ml/4 tbsp fresh lemon curd (recipe below right)

1 Preheat the oven to 190°C/375°F/Gas 5. Grease a 33 × 23cm/13 × 9in Swiss roll tin and line with non-stick baking paper.

2 In a large bowl, beat the egg yolks with half the caster sugar until light and foamy. Beat in the lemon rind and vanilla essence, then lightly fold in the ground almonds and flour using a large metal spoon or spatula.

3 Whisk the egg whites in a grease-free bowl until they form stiff, glossy peaks. Gradually whisk in the remaining caster sugar to form a stiff meringue. Stir half the meringue mixture into the egg yolk mixture and fold in the rest.

4 Pour into the prepared tin, level the surface with a palette knife and bake for 10 minutes or until risen and spongy to the touch. Cover loosely with a sheet of non-stick baking paper and a damp dish towel. Leave to cool in the tin.

5 Make the lemon cream. Whip the cream; then lightly fold in the lemon curd.

6 Sift the icing sugar liberally over a piece of non-stick baking paper. Turn the sponge out on to it. Peel off the lining paper and spread the lemon curd cream over the surface of the sponge, leaving a border around the edge.

7 Using the paper underneath as a guide, roll up the sponge from one of the long sides. Place on a serving platter, with the seam underneath. Cut the roulade into slices to serve.

FRESH LEMON CURD
Put the grated rind and juice of 3 lemons into a pan with 115g/4oz/½ cup caster sugar. Bring to the boil, stirring until the sugar has dissolved. Stir in 15ml/1 tbsp cornflour mixed to a paste with 15ml/1 tbsp cold water. Off the heat, whisk in 2 egg yolks. Return to a low heat, whisk for about 2 minutes; remove from the heat. Gradually whisk in 50g/2oz/¼ cup butter, at room temperature. Pour into a sterilized jar, cover and seal at once. Leave to cool, then chill. Use within 2–3 weeks. Makes 450g/1lb.

COOK'S TIP
Having filled and rolled the roulade, keep it wrapped in the non-stick baking paper and hold it together for about a minute to allow the shape to set before removing the paper and transferring the roulade to a plate.

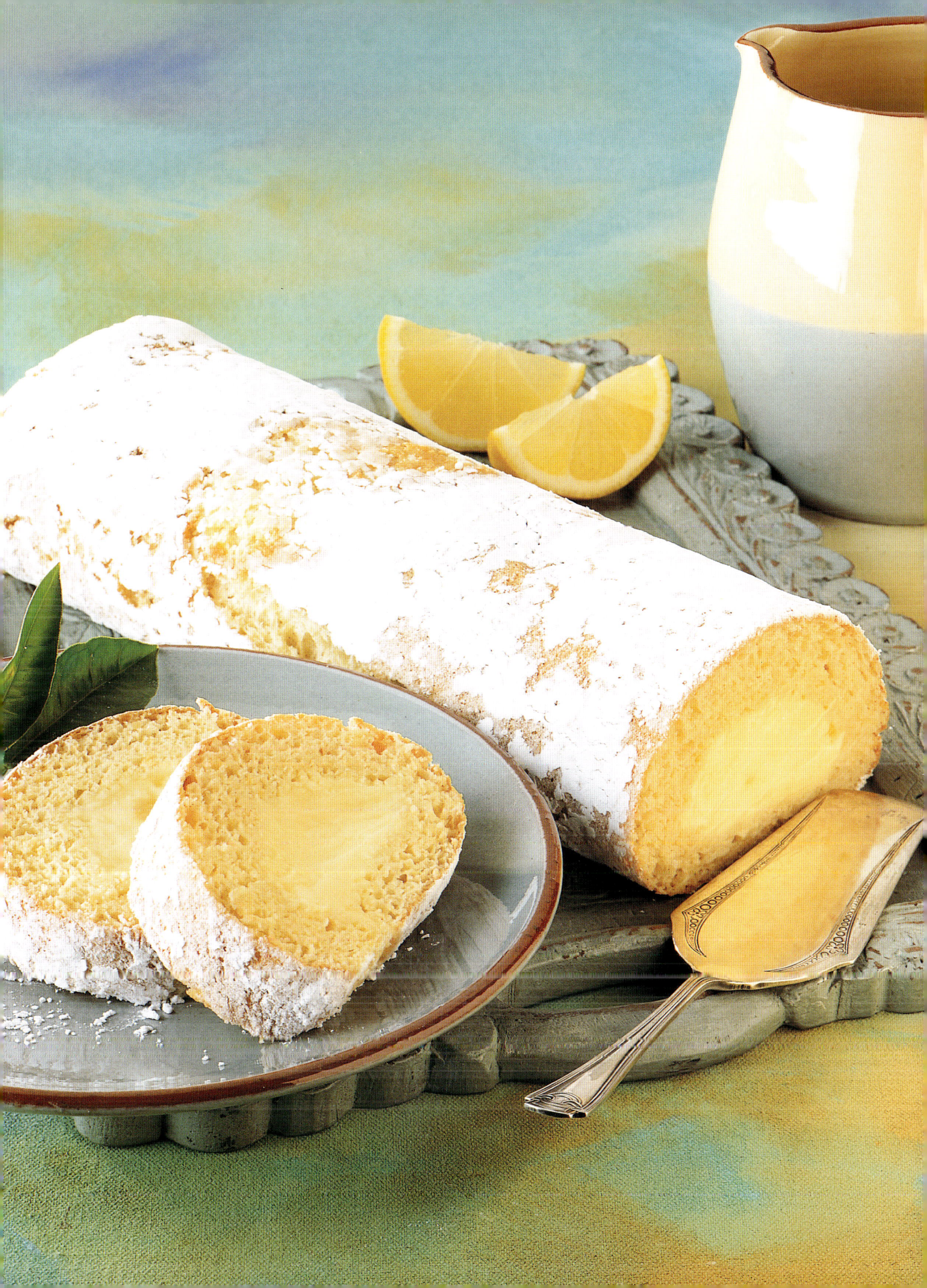

Lemon Meringue Pie

Crisp shortcrust is filled with a mouthwatering lemon cream filling and heaped with soft golden-topped meringue. This classic open tart never fails to please. Popular with adults and children, it is the essential Sunday lunch dessert.

SERVES SIX

INGREDIENTS
  115g/4oz/1 cup plain flour
  pinch of salt
  50g/2oz/¼ cup butter
  50g/2oz/¼ cup lard
  15ml/1 tbsp caster sugar
  about 15ml/1 tbsp iced water
For the filling
  3 large egg yolks
  30ml/2 tbsp caster sugar
  grated rind and juice of 1 lemon
  25g/1oz/½ cup fresh
    white breadcrumbs
  250ml/8fl oz/1 cup milk
For the topping
  3 large egg whites
  115g/4oz/½ cup caster sugar

1 Sift the flour and salt into a bowl. Rub in the butter and lard until the mixture resembles fine breadcrumbs. Stir in the sugar and add enough iced water to make a soft dough. Roll out the pastry on a lightly floured surface and line a 21cm/8½in pie plate or tin. Chill until required.

2 Meanwhile make the filling. Place all the ingredients in a bowl, mix lightly and leave to soak for 1 hour.

3 Preheat the oven to 200°C/400°F/Gas 6. Beat the filling until smooth and pour into the chilled pastry case. Bake for 20 minutes or until the filling has just set and the pastry is golden. Remove from the oven and cool on a wire rack for 30 minutes or until a skin has formed on the surface. Lower the oven temperature to 180°C/350°F/Gas 4.

4 Make the topping. Whisk the egg whites in a grease-free bowl until they form stiff peaks. Whisk in the caster sugar to form a glossy meringue. Spoon on top of the set lemon filling and spread over, making sure you spread the meringue right to the rim of the pie shell. Swirl the meringue slightly.

5 Bake the pie for 20–25 minutes or until the meringue is crisp and golden brown. Allow to cool on a wire rack for 10 minutes before serving.

Fresh Lemon Tart

Made famous by its French title – Tarte au Citron – this tart should be served at room temperature if the zesty lemon flavour is to be enjoyed to the full.

SERVES SIX TO EIGHT

INGREDIENTS
    350g/12oz packet ready-made rich
       sweet shortcrust pastry, thawed
       if frozen
For the filling
    3 eggs
    115g/4oz/½ cup caster sugar
    115g/4oz/1 cup ground almonds
    105ml/7 tbsp double cream
    grated rind and juice of 2 lemons
For the topping
    2 thin-skinned unwaxed lemons,
       thinly sliced
    200g/7oz/scant 1 cup caster sugar
    105ml/7 tbsp water

COOK'S TIP
If you prefer not to candy the lemons, simply dust the tart with icing sugar.

1 Roll out the pastry and line a deep 23cm/9in fluted flan tin. Prick the base and chill for 30 minutes.

2 Preheat the oven to 200°C/400°F/Gas 6. Line the pastry with non-stick baking paper and baking beans and bake blind for 10 minutes. Remove the paper and beans and return the pastry case to the oven for 5 minutes more.

3 Meanwhile, make the filling. Beat the eggs, caster sugar, almonds and cream in a bowl until smooth. Beat in the lemon rind and juice. Pour the filling into the pastry case. Lower the oven temperature to 190°C/375°F/Gas 5 and bake for 20 minutes or until the filling has set and the pastry is golden.

4 Make the topping. Place the lemon slices in a pan and pour over water to cover. Simmer for 15–20 minutes or until the skins are tender, then drain.

5 Place the sugar in a saucepan and stir in the measured water. Heat gently until the sugar has dissolved, stirring constantly, then boil for 2 minutes. Add the lemon slices and cook for 10–15 minutes until the skins become shiny and candied.

6 Lift out the candied lemon slices and arrange them over the top of the tart. Return the syrup to the heat and boil until reduced to a thick glaze. Brush this over the tart and allow to cool completely before serving.

Citrus Fruit Recipes

Key Lime Pie

THIS IS ONE OF AMERICA'S FAVOURITES. AS THE NAME SUGGESTS, IT ORIGINATED IN THE FLORIDA KEYS.

MAKES TEN SLICES

INGREDIENTS
225g/8oz/2 cups plain flour
115g/4oz/½ cup chilled
  butter, diced
30ml/2 tbsp caster sugar
2 egg yolks
pinch of salt
30ml/2 tbsp cold water
thinly pared lime rind and mint
  leaves, to decorate
For the filling
4 eggs, separated
400g/14oz can condensed milk
grated rind and juice of 3 limes
a few drops of green food
  colouring (optional)
30ml/2 tbsp caster sugar
For the topping
300ml/½ pint/1¼ cups double cream
2–3 limes, thinly sliced

1 Sift the flour into a mixing bowl and rub in the butter using your fingertips until the mixture resembles fresh breadcrumbs. Add the sugar, egg yolks, salt and water. Mix to a soft dough.

2 Roll out the pastry on a lightly floured surface and use to line a deep 21cm/8½in fluted flan tin, allowing the excess pastry to hang over the edge. Prick the pastry base and chill for at least 30 minutes.

3 Preheat the oven to 200°C/400°F/Gas 6. Trim off the excess pastry from around the edge of the pastry case using a large sharp knife and line the pastry case with non-stick baking paper and baking beans.

4 Bake the pastry case blind for 10 minutes. Remove the paper and beans and return the pastry case to the oven for 10 minutes.

5 Meanwhile, make the filling. Beat the egg yolks in a large bowl until light and creamy, then beat in the condensed milk, with the lime rind and juice until well combined. Add the food colouring, if using, and continue to beat until the mixture is thick.

COOK'S TIP
You can make the pastry in a food processor, but take care not to overprocess the dough. Use the pulse button and process for a few seconds at a time; switch off the motor the moment the dough clumps together.

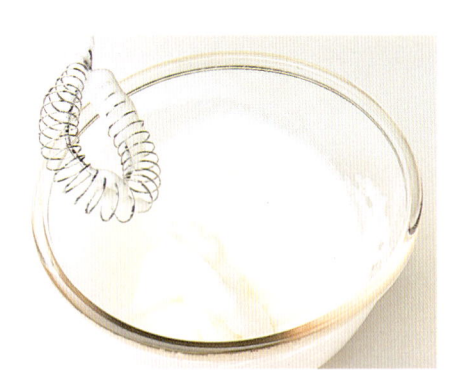

6 In a grease-free bowl, whisk the egg whites to stiff peaks. Whisk in the caster sugar, then fold into the lime mixture.

7 Lower the oven temperature to 160°C/325°F/Gas 3. Pour the lime filling into the pastry case. Bake for 20–25 minutes or until it has set and is starting to brown. Cool, then chill.

8 Just before serving, whip the double cream for the topping and spoon it around the edge of the pie. Cut the lime slices once from the centre to the edge, then twist each slice and arrange between the spoonfuls of cream. Decorate with lime rind and mint leaves.

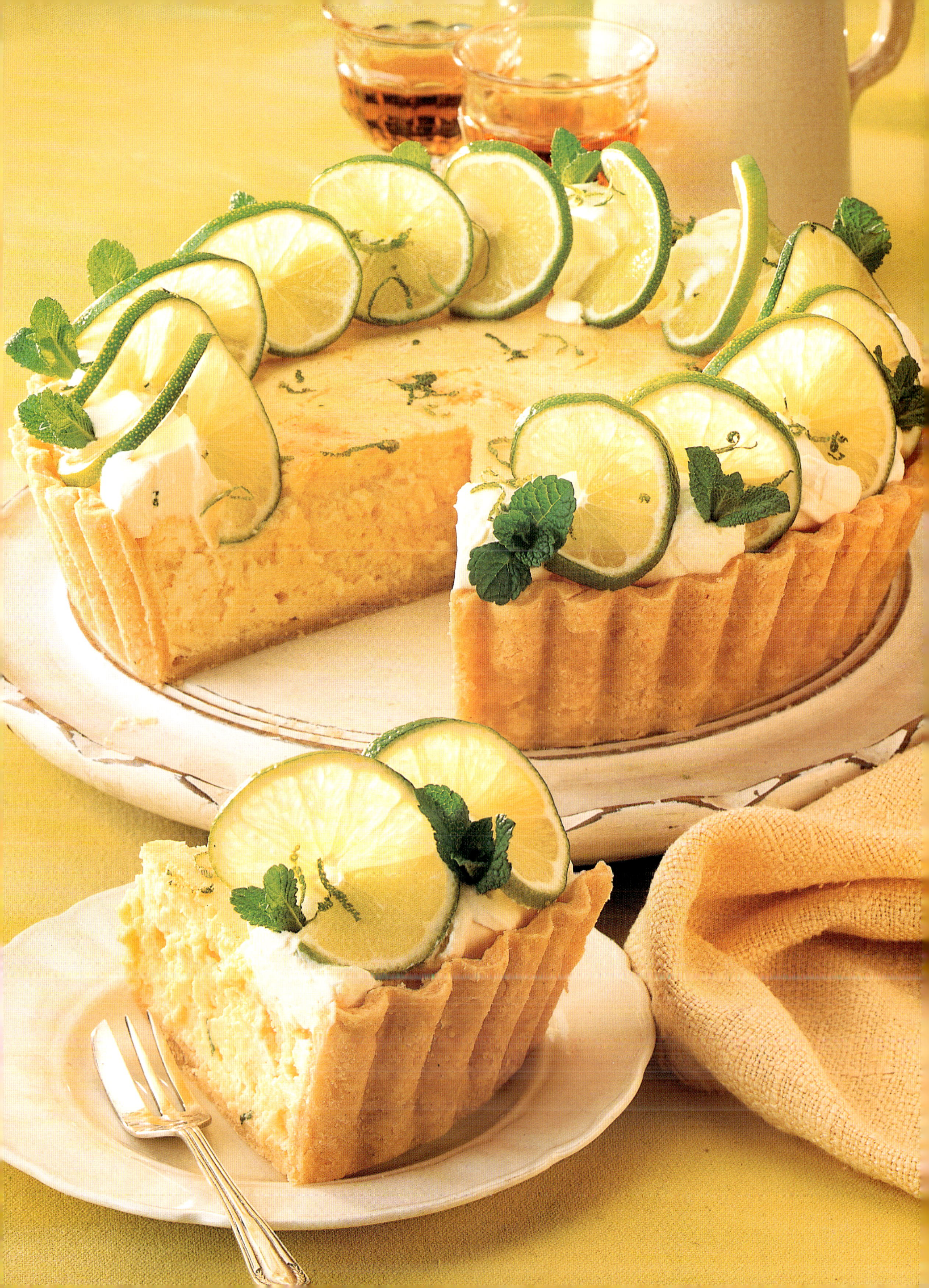

Moist Orange and Almond Cake

THE KEY TO THIS RECIPE IS TO COOK THE ORANGE SLOWLY FIRST, SO IT IS FULLY TENDER BEFORE BEING BLENDED. DON'T USE A MICROWAVE TO SPEED THINGS UP – THIS MAKES ORANGE SKIN TOUGH.

SERVES EIGHT

INGREDIENTS

- 1 large orange
- 3 eggs
- 225g/8oz/1 cup caster sugar
- 5ml/1 tsp baking powder
- 225g/8oz/2 cups ground almonds
- 25g/1oz/¼ cup plain flour
- icing sugar, for dusting
- whipped cream and orange slices (optional), to serve

1 Wash the orange and pierce it with a skewer. Put it in a deep saucepan and pour over water to cover completely. Bring to the boil then lower the heat, cover and simmer for 1 hour or until the skin is very soft. Drain, then cool.

COOK'S TIP
For a treat, serve this with spiced poached kumquats.

2 Preheat the oven to 180°C/350°F/Gas 4. Grease a 20cm/8in round cake tin and line it with non-stick baking paper. Cut the cooled orange in half and discard the pips. Place the orange, skin and all, in a blender or food processor and purée until smooth and pulpy.

3 In a bowl, whisk the eggs and sugar until thick. Fold in the baking powder, almonds and flour. Fold in the purée.

4 Pour into the prepared tin, level the surface and bake for 1 hour or until a skewer inserted into the middle comes out clean. Cool the cake in the tin for 10 minutes, then turn out on to a wire rack, peel off the lining paper and cool completely. Dust the top liberally with icing sugar and serve as a dessert with whipped cream. For added colour, tuck thick orange slices under the cake just before serving.

Citrus Fruit Recipes   85

Lemon and Lime Syrup Cake

THIS CAKE IS PERFECT FOR BUSY COOKS AS IT CAN BE MIXED IN MOMENTS AND NEEDS NO ICING. THE SIMPLE TANGY LIME TOPPING TRANSFORMS IT INTO A FABULOUSLY MOIST CAKE.

SERVES EIGHT

INGREDIENTS
225g/8oz/2 cups self-raising flour
5ml/1 tsp baking powder
225g/8oz/1 cup caster sugar
225g/8oz/1 cup butter, softened
4 eggs, beaten
grated rind of 2 lemons
30ml/2 tbsp lemon juice

For the topping
finely pared rind of 1 lime
juice of 2 limes
150g/5oz/⅔ cup caster sugar

1 Make the cake. Preheat the oven to 160°C/325°F/Gas 3. Grease and line a 20cm/8in round cake tin. Sift the flour and baking powder into a large bowl. Add the caster sugar, butter and eggs and beat together well until the mixture is smooth, creamy and fluffy.

2 Beat in the lemon rind and juice. Spoon the mixture into the prepared tin, then smooth the surface and make a shallow indentation in the top with the back of a spoon.

3 Bake for 1¼–1½ hours or until the cake is golden on top and spongy when lightly pressed, and a skewer inserted in the centre comes out clean.

4 Meanwhile, mix the topping ingredients together. As soon as the cake is cooked, remove it from the oven and pour the topping over the surface. Allow the cake to cool in the tin.

VARIATION
Use lemon rind and juice instead of lime for the topping if you prefer. You will need only one large lemon.

Spiced Poached Kumquats

KUMQUATS ARE NOT AVAILABLE THROUGHOUT THE YEAR, BUT THEY ARE UNDOUBTEDLY AT THEIR BEST JUST BEFORE THE CHRISTMAS SEASON. THESE FRUITS CAN BE BOTTLED AND GIVEN AS PRESENTS. THEIR MARVELLOUS SPICY-SWEET CITRUS FLAVOUR COMPLEMENTS BOTH SWEET AND SAVOURY DISHES.

SERVES SIX

INGREDIENTS
450g/1lb/4 cups kumquats
115g/4oz/½ cup caster sugar
150ml/¼ pint/⅔ cup water
1 small cinnamon stick
1 star anise
a citrus leaf, to decorate

1 Cut the kumquats in half and discard the pips. Place the kumquats in a saucepan with the sugar, water and spices. Cook over a gentle heat, stirring until the sugar has dissolved.

2 Increase the heat, cover the pan and boil the mixture for 8–10 minutes until the kumquats are tender. To bottle the kumquats, spoon them into warm, sterilized jars, seal and label.

3 If you want to serve the spiced kumquats soon after making them, let the mixture cool, then chill it. Decorate with a citrus leaf, if you like.

COOK'S TIP
Try these delectable treats with baked ham, roast pork or slices of a raised pork pie. They would also make a perfect accompaniment for moist almond or chocolate cake.

Three-fruit Marmalade

SEVILLE ORANGES HAVE A FINE FLAVOUR AND ARE THE BEST VARIETY FOR MARMALADE. SWEET ORANGES CAN BE USED AT A PINCH, BUT THEY TEND TO MAKE THE MARMALADE CLOUDY.

MAKES 2.25KG/5–5¼LB

INGREDIENTS
2 Seville oranges
2 lemons
1 grapefruit
1.75 litres/3 pints/7½ cups water
1.5kg/3lb 6oz/6¾ cups granulated sugar
croissants, to serve (optional)

1 Wash the fruit, halve and squeeze their juice. Pour into a large heavy-based saucepan or preserving pan. Tip the pips and pulp in a square of muslin, gather the sides into a bag and tie the neck tightly with string. Tie the bag to the handle of the pan so that it dangles in the citrus juice.

2 Cut the citrus skins into thin wedges; scrape off and discard the membranes and pith. Cut the rinds into slivers and add to the pan with the measured water. Bring to the simmer and cook gently for 2 hours until the rinds are very tender and the water has reduced by half. Test the rinds for softness by pressing a cooled piece with a finger.

3 Lift out the muslin bag, squeezing out the juice into the pan. Discard the bag. Stir the sugar into the pan and heat very gently, stirring occasionally, until all the sugar has dissolved.

4 Bring the mixture to the boil and boil for 10–15 minutes or until the marmalade registers 105°C/220°C.

5 Alternatively, test the marmalade for setting by pouring a small amount on to a chilled saucer. Chill for 2 minutes, then push the marmalade with your finger; if wrinkles form on the surface, it is ready. Cool for 15 minutes.

6 Stir the marmalade and pour it into warm, sterilized jars. Cover with waxed paper discs. Seal and label when cold. Store in a cool dark cupboard. Serve with warm croissants, if you like.

COOK'S TIP
Leaving the marmalade to cool slightly before potting lets it set enough to prevent the fruit from sinking. Stir before pouring it into the jars. Cover the surface with paper discs and seal while hot.

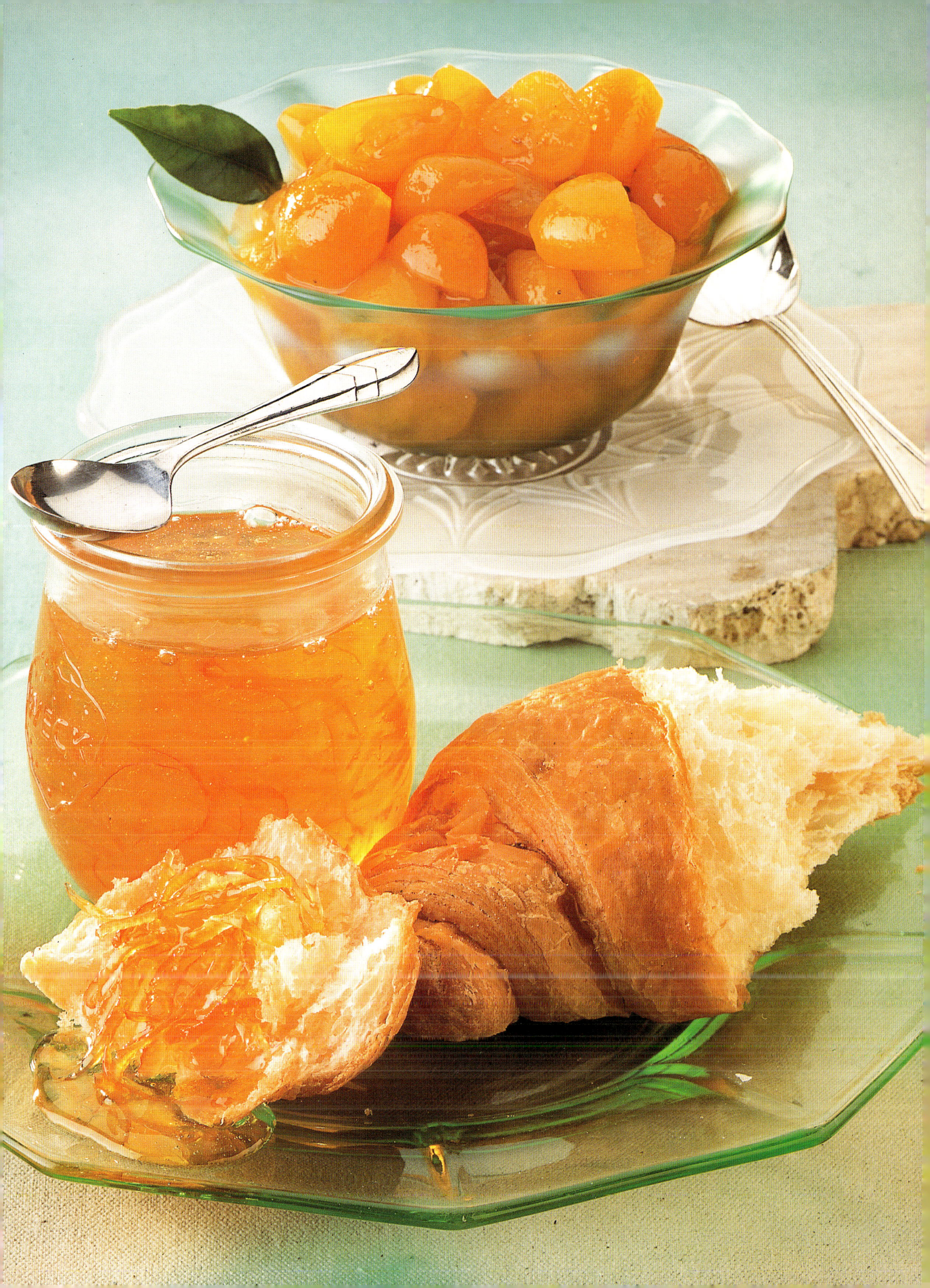

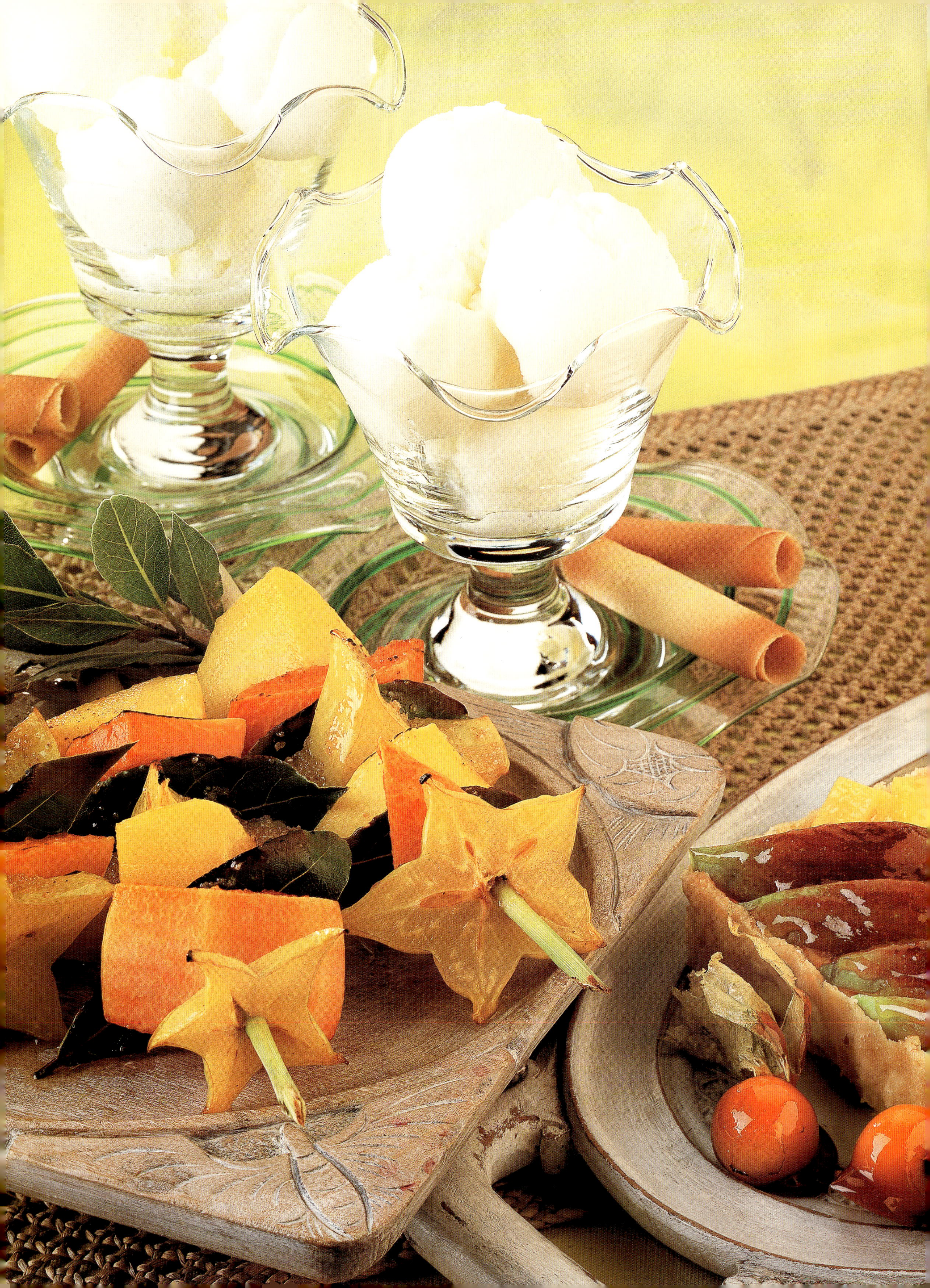

Exotic Fruit Recipes

Who can resist the colours, textures and flavours of exotic fruits? Now that many varieties are widely available all year, there's every excuse for taking the taste trip and trying such delights as Lychee and Elderflower Sorbet, Passion Fruit Crème Caramels with Dipped Physalis or Exotic Fruit Sushi.

Cold Mango Soufflés Topped with Toasted Coconut

Fragrant, fresh mango is one of the most delicious exotic fruits around, whether it is simply served in slices or used as the basis for an ice cream or soufflé.

MAKES FOUR

INGREDIENTS
- 4 small mangoes, peeled, stoned and chopped
- 30ml/2 tbsp water
- 15ml/1 tbsp powdered gelatine
- 2 egg yolks
- 115g/4oz/½ cup caster sugar
- 120ml/4fl oz/½ cup milk
- grated rind of 1 orange
- 300ml/½ pint/1¼ cups double cream
- toasted flaked or coarsely shredded coconut, to decorate

COOK'S TIP
Cool and creamy, these go down a treat after a curry. Add some juicy pieces of fresh mango on the side if you like.

1 Place a few pieces of mango in the base of each of four 150ml/¼ pint/⅔ cup ramekins. Wrap a greased collar of non-stick baking paper around the outside of each dish, extending well above the rim. Secure with adhesive tape, then tie tightly with string.

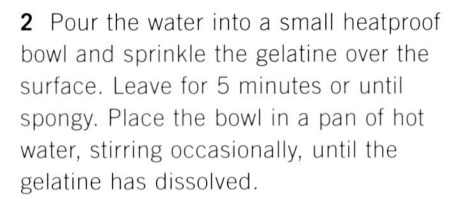

2 Pour the water into a small heatproof bowl and sprinkle the gelatine over the surface. Leave for 5 minutes or until spongy. Place the bowl in a pan of hot water, stirring occasionally, until the gelatine has dissolved.

3 Meanwhile, whisk the egg yolks with the caster sugar and milk in another heatproof bowl. Place the bowl over a saucepan of simmering water and continue to whisk until the mixture is thick and frothy. Remove from the heat and continue whisking until the mixture cools. Whisk in the liquid gelatine.

4 Purée the remaining mango pieces in a food processor or blender, then fold the purée into the egg yolk mixture with the orange rind. Set the mixture aside until starting to thicken.

5 Whip the double cream to soft peaks. Reserve 60ml/4 tbsp and fold the rest into the mango mixture. Spoon into the ramekins until the mixture is 2.5cm/1in above the rim of each dish. Chill for 3–4 hours or until set.

6 Carefully remove the paper collars from the soufflés. Spoon a little of the reserved cream on top of each soufflé and decorate with some toasted flaked or coarsely shredded coconut.

Passion Fruit Crème Caramels with Dipped Physalis

Passion fruit has an aromatic flavour that really permeates these crème caramels. Use some of the caramel to dip physalis to create a unique decoration.

MAKES FOUR

INGREDIENTS
- 185g/6½oz/generous ¾ cup caster sugar
- 75ml/5 tbsp water
- 4 passion fruit
- 4 physalis
- 3 eggs plus 1 egg yolk
- 150ml/¼ pint/⅔ cup double cream
- 150ml/¼ pint/⅔ cup creamy milk

1 Place 150g/5oz/⅔ cup of the caster sugar in a heavy-based saucepan. Add the water and heat the mixture gently until the sugar has dissolved. Increase the heat and boil until the syrup turns a dark golden colour.

2 Meanwhile, cut each passion fruit in half. Scoop out the seeds from the passion fruit into a sieve set over a bowl. Press the seeds against the sieve to extract all their juice. Spoon a few of the seeds into each of four 150ml/¼ pint/⅔ cup ramekins. Set the juice aside.

3 Peel back the papery casing from each physalis and dip the orange berries into the caramel. Place on a sheet of non-stick baking paper and set aside. Pour the remaining caramel carefully into the ramekins.

4 Preheat the oven to 150°C/300°F/Gas 2. Whisk the eggs, egg yolk and remaining sugar in a bowl. Whisk in the cream and milk, then the passion fruit juice. Strain through a sieve into each ramekin, then place the ramekins in a baking tin. Pour in hot water to come halfway up the sides of the dishes; bake for 40–45 minutes or until just set.

5 Remove the custards from the tin and leave to cool, then cover and chill them for 4 hours before serving. Run a knife between the edge of each ramekin and the custard and invert each in turn on to a dessert plate. Shake the ramekins firmly to release the custards. Decorate each with a dipped physalis.

Lychee and Elderflower Sorbet

The flavour of elderflowers is famous for bringing out the essence of gooseberries, but what is less well known is how wonderfully it complements lychees.

SERVES FOUR

INGREDIENTS
- 175g/6oz/¾ cup caster sugar
- 400ml/14fl oz/1⅔ cups water
- 500g/1¼lb fresh lychees, peeled and stoned
- 15ml/1 tbsp elderflower cordial
- dessert biscuits, to serve

COOK'S TIP
Switch the freezer to the coldest setting before making the sorbet – the faster the mixture freezes, the smaller the ice crystals that form and the better the final texture will be. To ensure rapid freezing, use a metal freezerproof container and place it directly on the freezer shelf.

1 Place the sugar and water in a saucepan and heat gently until the sugar has dissolved. Increase the heat and boil for 5 minutes, then add the lychees. Lower the heat and simmer for 7 minutes. Remove from the heat and allow to cool.

2 Purée the fruit and syrup in a blender or food processor. Place a sieve over a bowl and pour the purée into it. Press through as much of the purée as possible with a spoon.

3 Stir the elderflower cordial into the strained purée, then pour the mixture into a freezerproof container. Freeze for 2 hours, until ice crystals start to form around the edges.

4 Remove the sorbet from the freezer and process briefly in a food processor or blender to break up the crystals. Repeat this process twice more, then freeze until firm. Transfer to the fridge for 10 minutes to soften slightly before serving in scoops, with biscuits.

Exotic Fruit Sushi

This idea can be adapted to incorporate a wide variety of fruits, but to keep to the exotic theme take your inspiration from the tropics. The sushi needs to chill overnight to ensure the rice mixture firms properly, so be sure you start this in good time.

SERVES FOUR

INGREDIENTS

- 150g/5oz/⅔ cup short grain pudding rice
- 350ml/12fl oz/1½ cups water
- 400ml/14fl oz/1⅔ cups coconut milk
- 75g/3oz/⅓ cup caster sugar
- a selection of exotic fruit, such as 1 mango, 1 kiwi fruit, 2 figs and 1 star fruit, thinly sliced
- 30ml/2 tbsp apricot jam, sieved

For the raspberry sauce
- 225g/8oz/2 cups raspberries
- 25g/1oz/¼ cup icing sugar

COOK'S TIP
To cut the rice mixture into bars, turn out of the tin, cut in half lengthways, then make 7 crossways cuts for 16 bars. Shape into ovals with damp hands.

1 Rinse the rice well under cold running water, drain and place in a saucepan with 300ml/½ pint/1¼ cups of the water. Pour in 175ml/6fl oz/¾ cup of the coconut milk. Cook over a very low heat for 25 minutes, stirring often and gradually adding the remaining coconut milk, until the rice has absorbed all the liquid and is tender.

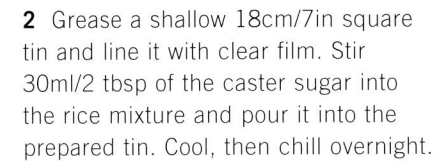

2 Grease a shallow 18cm/7in square tin and line it with clear film. Stir 30ml/2 tbsp of the caster sugar into the rice mixture and pour it into the prepared tin. Cool, then chill overnight.

3 Cut the rice mixture into 16 small bars, shape into ovals and flatten the tops. Place on a baking sheet lined with non-stick baking paper. Arrange the sliced fruit on top, using one type of fruit only for each sushi.

4 Place the remaining sugar in a small pan with the remaining 50ml/4 tbsp water. Bring to the boil, then lower the heat and simmer until thick and syrupy. Stir in the jam and cool slightly.

5 To make the sauce, purée the raspberries with the icing sugar in a food processor or blender. Press through a sieve, then divide among four small bowls. Arrange a few different fruit sushi on each plate and spoon over a little of the cool apricot syrup. Serve with the sauce.

Lemon Grass Skewers with Lime Cheese

Grilled fruits make a fine finale to a barbecue, whether they are cooked over the coals or under a hot grill. The lemon grass skewers give the fruit a subtle lemon tang. The fruits used here make an ideal exotic mix, but almost any soft fruit can be substituted.

SERVES FOUR

INGREDIENTS
- 4 long fresh lemon grass stalks
- 1 mango, peeled, stoned and cut into chunks
- 1 papaya, peeled, seeded and cut into chunks
- 1 star fruit, cut into thick slices and halved
- 8 fresh bay leaves
- a nutmeg
- 60ml/4 tbsp maple syrup
- 50g/2oz/⅓ cup demerara sugar

For the lime cheese
- 150g/5oz/⅔ cup curd cheese or low fat soft cheese
- 120ml/4fl oz/½ cup double cream
- grated rind and juice of ½ lime
- 30ml/2 tbsp icing sugar

1 Prepare the barbecue or preheat the grill. Cut the top of each lemon grass stalk into a point with a sharp knife. Discard the outer leaves, then use the back of the knife to bruise the length of each stalk to release the aromatic oils. Thread each stalk, skewer-style, with the fruit pieces and bay leaves.

2 Support a piece of foil on a baking sheet and roll up the edges to make a rim. Grease the foil, lay the kebabs on top and grate a little nutmeg over each. Drizzle the maple syrup over and dust liberally with the demerara sugar. Grill for 5 minutes, until lightly charred.

3 Meanwhile, make the lime cheese. Mix together the cheese, cream, grated lime rind and juice and icing sugar in a bowl. Serve at once with the lightly charred fruit kebabs.

COOK'S TIP
Only fresh lemon grass will work as skewers for this recipe. It is now possible to buy lemon grass stalks in jars. These are handy for curries and similar dishes, but are too soft to use as skewers.

Coconut Jelly with Star Anise Fruits

Serve this dessert after any oriental-style meal with plenty of refreshing exotic fruit.

SERVES FOUR

INGREDIENTS
- 250ml/8fl oz/1 cup cold water
- 75g/3oz/⅓ cup caster sugar
- 15ml/1 tbsp powdered gelatine
- 400ml/14fl oz/1⅔ cups coconut milk

For the syrup and fruit
- 250ml/8fl oz/1 cup water
- 3 star anise
- 50g/2oz/¼ cup caster sugar
- 1 star fruit, sliced
- 12 lychees, peeled and stoned
- 115g/4oz/1 cup blackberries

1 Pour the water into a saucepan and add the caster sugar. Heat gently until the sugar has dissolved. Sprinkle over the gelatine and continue to heat the mixture gently until the gelatine has dissolved, stirring occasionally. Stir in the coconut milk, remove from the heat and set aside to cool.

2 Grease an 18cm/7in square cake tin. Line with clear film. Pour in the coconut milk mixture and chill until set.

3 To make the syrup, combine the water, star anise and sugar in a pan. Bring to the boil, stirring, then lower the heat and simmer for 10–12 minutes until syrupy. Place the fruit in a heatproof bowl and pour over the hot syrup. Cool, then chill.

4 To serve, cut the coconut jelly into diamonds and remove from the tin. Arrange the coconut jelly on individual plates, adding a few of the fruits and their syrup to each portion.

COOK'S TIP
Coconut milk is available in cans or as a powder. If using the powder, reconstitute it with cold water according to the packet instructions.

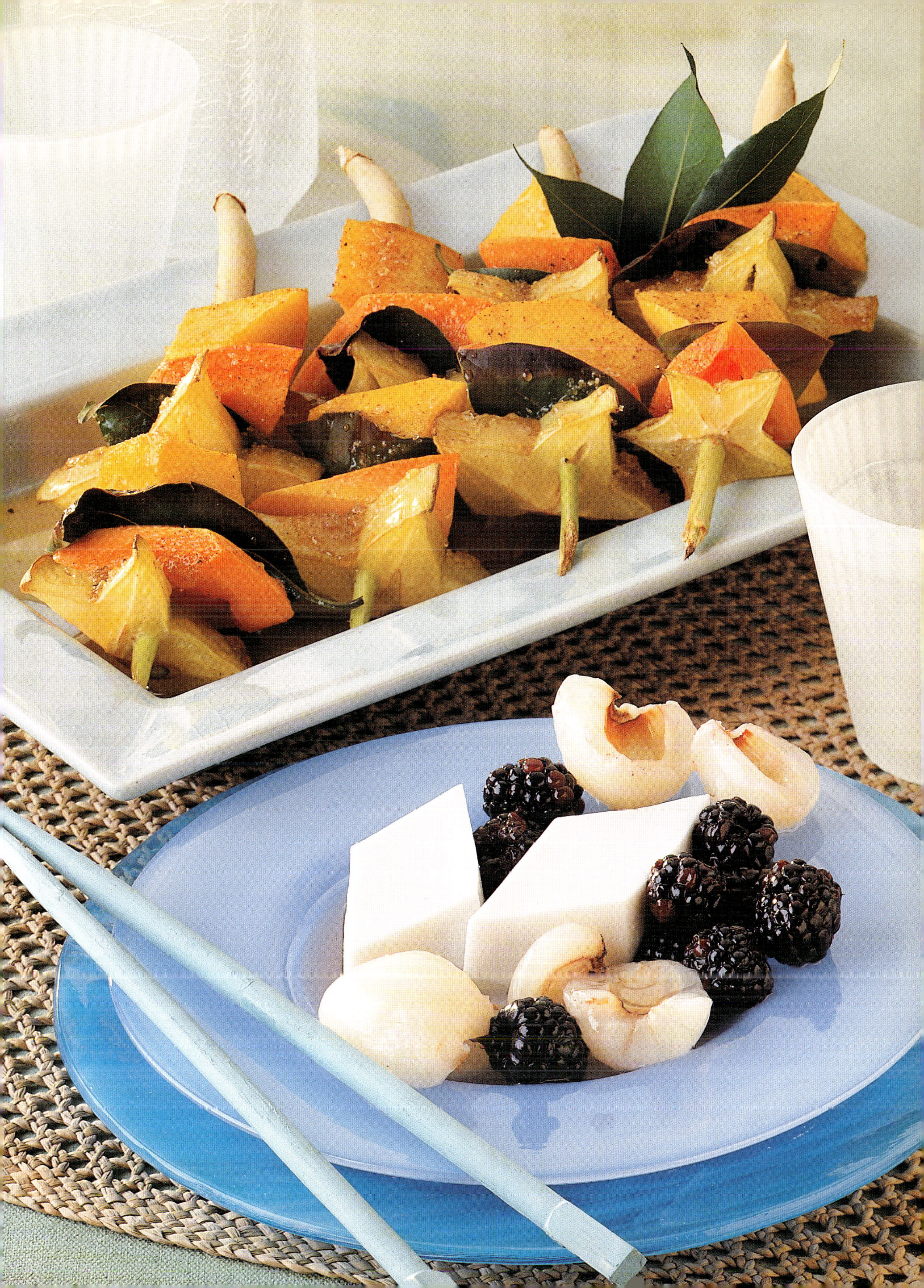

Papaya Baked with Ginger

Ginger enhances the flavour of papaya in this recipe, which takes no more than ten minutes to prepare! Don't overcook papaya or the flesh will become very watery.

SERVES FOUR

INGREDIENTS

2 ripe papayas
2 pieces stem ginger in syrup, drained, plus 15ml/1 tbsp syrup from the jar
8 amaretti or other dessert biscuits, coarsely crushed
45ml/3 tbsp raisins
shredded, finely pared rind and juice of 1 lime
25g/1oz/¼ cup pistachio nuts, chopped
15ml/1 tbsp light muscovado sugar
60ml/4 tbsp crème fraîche, plus extra to serve

VARIATION
Use Greek yogurt and almonds instead of crème fraîche and pistachios.

1 Preheat the oven to 200°C/400°F/Gas 6. Cut the papayas in half and scoop out their seeds. Place the halves in a baking dish and set aside. Cut the stem ginger into fine matchsticks.

2 Make the filling. Combine the crushed amaretti biscuits, stem ginger matchsticks and raisins in a bowl.

3 Stir in the lime rind and juice, two thirds of the nuts, then add the sugar and the crème fraîche. Mix well.

4 Fill the papaya halves and drizzle with the ginger syrup. Sprinkle with the remaining nuts. Bake for about 25 minutes or until tender. Serve with extra crème fraîche.

Exotic Fruit Salad with Passion Fruit Dressing

Passion fruit makes a superb dressing for any fruit, but really brings out the flavour of exotic varieties. You can easily double the recipe, then serve the rest for breakfast.

SERVES SIX

INGREDIENTS

1 mango
1 papaya
2 kiwi fruit
coconut or vanilla ice cream, to serve

For the dressing
3 passion fruit
thinly pared rind and juice of 1 lime
5ml/1 tsp hazelnut or walnut oil
15ml/1 tbsp clear honey

COOK'S TIP
A clear golden honey scented with orange blossom or acacia blossom would be perfect for the dressing.

1 Peel the mango, cut it into three slices, then cut the flesh into chunks and place it in a large bowl. Peel the papaya and cut it in half. Scoop out the seeds, then chop the flesh.

2 Cut both ends off each kiwi fruit, then stand them on a board. Using a small sharp knife, cut off the skin from top to bottom. Cut each kiwi fruit in half lengthways, then cut into thick slices. Combine all the fruit in a large bowl.

3 Make the dressing. Cut each passion fruit in half and scoop the seeds out into a sieve set over a small bowl. Press the seeds well to extract all their juices. Lightly whisk the remaining dressing ingredients into the passion fruit juice, then pour the dressing over the fruit. Mix gently to combine. Leave to chill for 1 hour before serving with scoops of coconut or vanilla ice cream.

Tropical Fruit Gratin

This out-of-the-ordinary gratin is strictly for grown-ups. A colourful combination of fruit is topped with a simple sabayon before being flashed under the grill.

SERVES FOUR

INGREDIENTS
2 tamarillos
½ sweet pineapple
1 ripe mango
175g/6oz/1½ cups blackberries
120ml/4fl oz/½ cup sparkling white wine
115g/4oz/½ cup caster sugar
6 egg yolks

VARIATION
Although boiling drives off the alcohol in the wine, children do not always appreciate the flavour, so substitute orange juice if making the gratin for them. White grape juice or pineapple juice would also work well.

1 Cut each tamarillo in half lengthways and then into thick slices. Cut the rind and core from the pineapple and take spiral slices off the outside to remove the eyes. Cut the flesh into chunks. Peel the mango, cut it in half and cut the flesh from the stone in slices.

2 Divide all the fruit, including the blackberries, among four 14cm/5½in gratin dishes set on a baking sheet and set aside. Heat the wine and sugar in a saucepan until the sugar has dissolved. Bring to the boil and cook for 5 minutes.

3 Put the egg yolks in a large heatproof bowl. Place the bowl over a pan of simmering water and whisk until pale. Slowly pour on the hot sugar syrup, whisking all the time, until the mixture thickens. Preheat the grill.

4 Spoon the mixture over the fruit. Place the baking sheet holding the dishes on a low shelf under the hot grill until the topping is golden. Serve hot.

Grilled Pineapple with Papaya Sauce

Pineapple cooked this way takes on a superb flavour and is sensational when served with the papaya sauce.

SERVES SIX

INGREDIENTS
1 sweet pineapple
melted butter, for greasing and brushing
2 pieces drained stem ginger in syrup, cut into fine matchsticks, plus 30ml/2 tbsp of the syrup from the jar
30ml/2 tbsp demerara sugar
pinch of ground cinnamon
fresh mint sprigs, to decorate

For the sauce
1 ripe papaya, peeled and seeded
175ml/6fl oz/¾ cup apple juice

1 Peel the pineapple and take spiral slices off the outside to remove the eyes. Cut it crossways into six slices, each 2.5cm/1in thick. Line a baking sheet with a sheet of foil, rolling up the sides to make a rim. Grease the foil with melted butter. Preheat the grill.

2 Arrange the pineapple slices on the lined baking sheet. Brush with butter, then top with the ginger matchsticks, sugar and cinnamon. Drizzle over the stem ginger syrup. Grill for 5–7 minutes or until the slices are golden and lightly charred on top.

3 Meanwhile, make the sauce. Cut a few slices from the papaya and set aside, then purée the rest with the apple juice in a blender or food processor.

4 Press the purée through a sieve placed over a bowl, then stir in any juices from cooking the pineapple. Serve the pineapple slices with a little sauce drizzled around each plate. Decorate with the reserved papaya slices and the mint sprigs.

COOK'S TIP
Try the papaya sauce with savoury dishes, too. It tastes great with grilled chicken and game birds as well as pork and lamb.

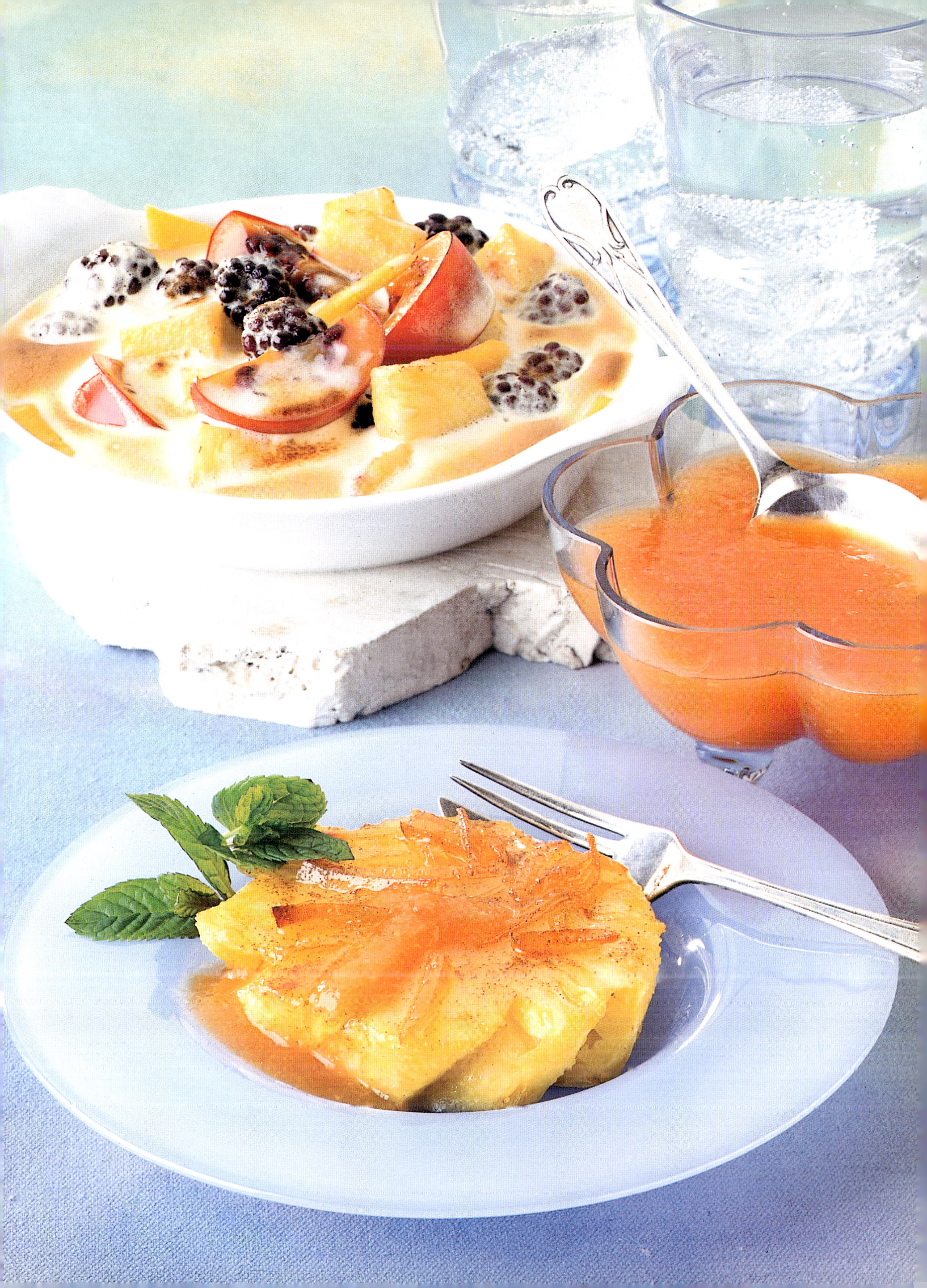

Jamaican Fruit Trifle

This trifle is actually based on a Caribbean fool that consists of fruit stirred into thick vanilla-flavoured cream. This version is much less rich, redressing the balance with plenty of fruit, and with crème fraîche replacing some of the cream.

SERVES EIGHT

INGREDIENTS

1 large sweet pineapple, peeled and cored, about 350g/12oz
300ml/½ pint/1¼ cups double cream
200ml/7fl oz/scant 1 cup crème fraîche
60ml/4 tbsp icing sugar, sifted
10ml/2 tsp pure vanilla essence
30ml/2 tbsp white or coconut rum
3 papayas, peeled, seeded and chopped
3 mangoes, peeled, stoned and chopped
thinly pared rind and juice of 1 lime
25g/1oz/⅓ cup coarsely shredded or flaked coconut, toasted

1 Cut the pineapple into large chunks, place in a food processor or blender and process briefly until chopped. Tip into a sieve placed over a bowl and leave for 5 minutes so that most of the juice drains from the fruit.

2 Whip the double cream to very soft peaks, then lightly but thoroughly fold in the crème fraîche, sifted icing sugar, vanilla essence and rum.

3 Fold the drained chopped pineapple into the cream mixture. Place the chopped papayas and mangoes in a large bowl and pour over the lime juice. Gently stir the fruit mixture to combine. Shred the pared lime rind.

4 Divide the fruit mixture and the pineapple cream among eight dessert plates. Decorate with the lime shreds, toasted coconut and a few small pineapple leaves, if you like, and serve at once.

COOK'S TIP

It is important to let the pineapple purée drain thoroughly, otherwise, the pineapple cream will be watery. Don't throw away the drained pineapple juice – mix it with fizzy mineral water for a refreshing drink.

Exotic Fruit Recipes 101

POMEGRANATE JEWELLED CHEESECAKE

THIS LIGHT CHEESECAKE IS FLAVOURED WITH COCONUT AND HAS A STUNNING POMEGRANATE GLAZE.

SERVES EIGHT

INGREDIENTS
    225g/8oz oat biscuits
    75g/3oz/⅓ cup unsalted
        butter, melted
For the filling
    45ml/3 tbsp orange juice
    15ml/1 tbsp powdered gelatine
    250g/9oz/generous 1 cup mascarpone
        cheese
    200g/7oz/scant 1 cup full fat
        soft cheese
    75g/3oz/¾ cup icing sugar, sifted
    200ml/7fl oz/scant 1 cup coconut
        cream
    2 egg whites
For the topping
    2 pomegranates, peeled and
        seeds separated
    grated rind and juice of 1 orange
    30ml/2 tbsp caster sugar
    15ml/1 tbsp arrowroot, mixed to a
        paste with 30ml/2 tbsp Kirsch
    a few drops of red food colouring
        (optional)

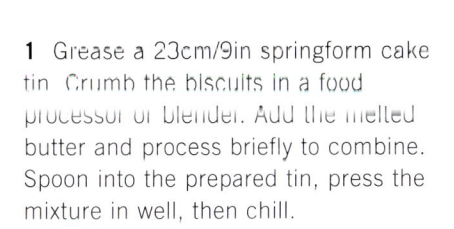

1 Grease a 23cm/9in springform cake tin. Crumb the biscuits in a food processor or blender. Add the melted butter and process briefly to combine. Spoon into the prepared tin, press the mixture in well, then chill.

COOK'S TIP
If you do not have a blender or food processor, crumb the biscuits by placing them in a large, strong plastic bag and crushing them with a rolling pin. For the best results, crush the crumbs as finely as possible.

2 For the filling, pour the orange juice into a heatproof bowl, sprinkle the gelatine on top and set aside for 5 minutes until sponged. Place the bowl in a pan of hot water and stir until the gelatine has dissolved.

3 In a bowl, beat together both cheeses and the icing sugar, then gradually beat in the coconut cream. Whisk the egg whites in a grease-free bowl to soft peaks. Quickly stir the melted gelatine into the coconut mixture and fold in the egg whites. Pour over the biscuit base, level and chill until set.

4 Make the cheesecake topping. Place the pomegranate seeds in a saucepan and add the orange rind and juice and caster sugar. Bring to the boil, then lower the heat, cover and simmer for 5 minutes. Add the arrowroot paste and heat, stirring constantly, until thickened. Stir in the food colouring, if using. Allow to cool, stirring occasionally.

5 Pour the glaze over the top of the set cheesecake, then chill. To serve, run a knife between the edge of the tin and the cheesecake, then remove the side of the tin.

Banana and Mascarpone Creams

If you are a fan of cold banana custard, you'll love this recipe. It is a grown-up version of an old favourite. No one will guess that the secret is ready-made custard sauce.

SERVES FOUR TO SIX

INGREDIENTS
250g/9oz/generous 1 cup mascarpone cheese
300ml/½ pint/1¼ cups fresh ready-made custard sauce
150ml/¼ pint/⅔ cup Greek yogurt
4 bananas
juice of 1 lime
50g/2oz/½ cup pecan nuts, coarsely chopped
120ml/4fl oz/½ cup maple syrup

VARIATION
Use clear honey instead of maple syrup and walnuts instead of pecans, if you like. Also, try layering in some crumbled biscuits, such as amaretti or ratafia, shortbread crumbs or crushed meringues. Or add a handful of finely grated dark or white chocolate.

1 Combine the mascarpone, custard sauce and yogurt in a large bowl and beat together until smooth. Make this mixture up to several hours ahead, if you like. Cover and chill, then stir before using.

2 Slice the bananas diagonally and place in a separate bowl. Pour over the lime juice and toss together until the bananas are coated in the juice.

3 Divide half the custard mixture among four or six dessert glasses and top each portion with a generous spoonful of the banana mixture.

4 Spoon the remaining custard mixture into the glasses and top with the rest of the bananas. Scatter the nuts over the top. Drizzle maple syrup over each dessert and chill for 30 minutes before serving.

Bananas with Lime and Cardamom Sauce

Serve these bananas solo, with vanilla ice cream, or spoon them over folded crêpes.

SERVES FOUR

INGREDIENTS
6 small bananas
50g/2oz/¼ cup butter
seeds from 4 cardamom pods, crushed
50g/2oz/½ cup flaked almonds
thinly pared rind and juice of 2 limes
50g/2oz/⅓ cup light muscovado sugar
30ml/2 tbsp dark rum
vanilla ice cream, to serve

VARIATION
If you prefer not to use alcohol in your cooking, replace the rum with orange juice or even pineapple juice.

1 Peel the bananas and cut them in half lengthways. Heat half the butter in a large frying pan. Add half the bananas, and cook until the undersides are golden. Turn carefully, using a fish slice. Cook until golden.

2 As they cook, transfer the bananas to a heatproof serving dish. Cook the remaining bananas in the same way.

3 Melt the remaining butter, then add the cardamom seeds and almonds. Cook, stirring until golden.

4 Stir in the lime rind and juice, then the sugar. Cook, stirring, until the mixture is smooth, bubbling and slightly reduced. Stir in the rum. Pour the sauce over the bananas and serve immediately, with vanilla ice cream.

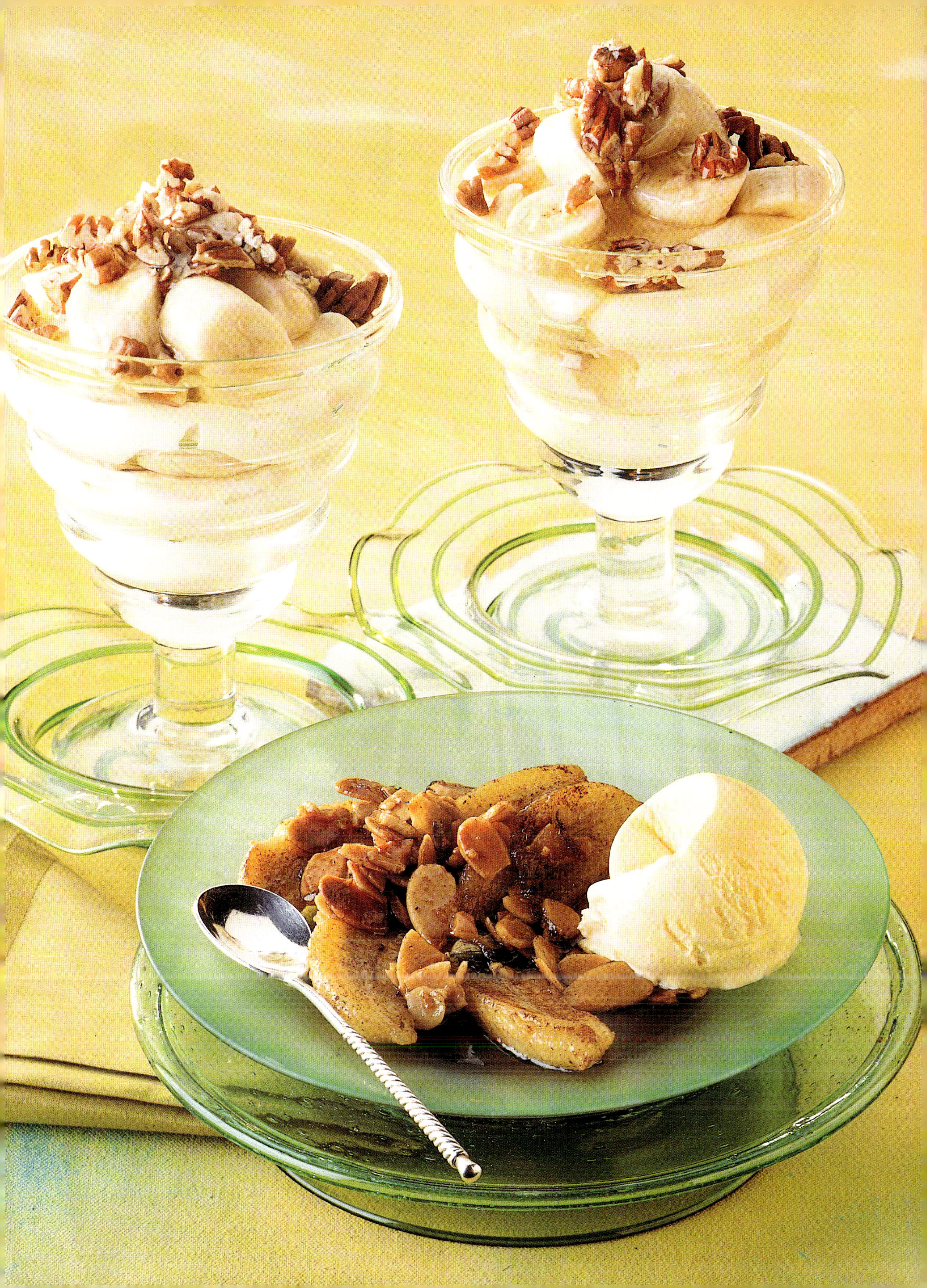

Toffee Bananas

Although the method for this recipe sounds simple, it can be a bit tricky to master. You need to work fast, especially when dipping the fruit in the caramel, as it will cool and set quite quickly. The luscious results, however, are worth the effort.

SERVES FOUR

INGREDIENTS

4 firm bananas
75g/3oz/¾ cup plain flour
50g/2oz/½ cup cornflour
10ml/2 tsp baking powder
175ml/6fl oz/¾ cup water
5ml/1 tsp sesame oil
groundnut, sunflower or corn oil, for deep frying

For the caramel
225g/8oz/1 cup granulated sugar
30ml/2 tbsp sesame seeds
60ml/4 tbsp water

1 Peel the bananas, then cut them diagonally into thick slices. Sift the flours and baking powder into a large bowl. Quickly beat in the water and sesame oil, taking care not to overmix. Stir in the bananas until coated.

2 Heat the groundnut, sunflower or corn oil in a deep pan until it registers 180°C/350°F or until a cube of bread, added to the oil, turns pale brown in 45 seconds.

3 Using a fork, remove a piece of banana from the batter, allowing the excess batter to drain back into the bowl. Gently lower the piece of banana into the hot oil. Add more pieces of battered banana in the same way; do not overcrowd the pan. Fry for about 2 minutes or until the coating is golden.

4 As they are cooked, remove the banana fritters from the oil with a slotted spoon and place on kitchen paper to drain. Cook the rest of the battered bananas in the same way.

5 When all the banana pieces have been fried, make the caramel. Mix the sugar, sesame seeds and water in a pan. Heat gently, stirring occasionally, until the sugar has dissolved. Raise the heat slightly and continue cooking, without stirring, until the syrup becomes a light caramel. Remove from the heat.

6 Have ready a bowl of iced water. Working quickly, drop one fritter at a time into the hot caramel. Flip over with a fork, remove immediately and plunge the piece into the iced water. Remove from the water quickly (using your fingers for speed, but taking care) and drain on a wire rack while coating the rest. Serve immediately.

Hot Date Puddings with Toffee Sauce

Fresh dates make this pudding less rich than the conventional dried date version, but it is still a bit of an indulgence! It is preferable to peel the dates as they can be rather tough: simply squeeze them between your thumb and forefinger and the skins will pop off.

SERVES SIX

INGREDIENTS
- 50g/2oz/¼ cup butter, softened
- 75g/3oz/½ cup light muscovado sugar
- 2 eggs, beaten
- 115g/4oz/1 cup self-raising flour
- 2.5ml/½ tsp bicarbonate of soda
- 175g/6oz/1 cup fresh dates, peeled, stoned and chopped
- 75ml/5 tbsp boiling water
- 10ml/2 tsp coffee and chicory essence

For the toffee sauce
- 75g/3oz/½ cup light muscovado sugar
- 50g/2oz/¼ cup butter
- 60ml/4 tbsp double cream
- 30ml/2 tbsp brandy

1 Preheat the oven to 180°C/350°F/Gas 4. Place a baking sheet in the oven to heat up. Grease six individual pudding moulds or tins. Cream the butter and sugar in a mixing bowl until pale and fluffy. Gradually add the eggs, beating well after each addition.

2 Sift the flour and bicarbonate of soda together and fold into the creamed mixture. Put the dates in a heatproof bowl, pour over the boiling water and mash with a potato masher. Add the coffee and chicory essence, then stir the paste into the creamed mixture.

3 Spoon the mixture into the prepared moulds or tins. Place on the hot baking sheet and bake for 20 minutes.

4 Meanwhile, make the toffee sauce. Put all the ingredients in a pan and heat very gently, stirring occasionally, until the mixture is smooth. Increase the heat and boil for 1 minute.

5 Turn the warm puddings out on to individual dessert plates. Spoon a generous amount of sauce over each portion and serve at once.

COOK'S TIP
The sauce is a great standby. Try it on poached apple or pear slices, over ice cream or with a steamed pudding.

Rum and Banana Waffles

To save time, these scrumptious dessert waffles can be made in advance, wrapped tightly, frozen, and then warmed through in the oven just before serving.

SERVES FOUR

INGREDIENTS
   225g/8oz/2 cups plain flour
   10ml/2 tsp baking powder
   5ml/1 tsp bicarbonate of soda
   15ml/1 tbsp caster sugar
   2 eggs
   50g/2oz/¼ cup butter, melted
   175ml/6fl oz/¾ cup milk, plus
      additional if needed
   300ml/½ pint/1¼ cups buttermilk
   5ml/1 tsp pure vanilla essence
   single cream, to serve
For the bananas
   6 bananas, thickly sliced
   115g/4oz/1 cup pecan nuts, broken
      into pieces
   50g/2oz/⅓ cup demerara sugar
   75ml/5 tbsp maple syrup
   45ml/3 tbsp dark rum

1 Sift the dry ingredients into a large mixing bowl. Make a well in the centre. Add the eggs, melted butter and milk. Whisk together, gradually incorporating the flour mixture, until smooth.

2 Add the buttermilk and vanilla to the batter and whisk well. Cover and leave to stand for 30 minutes. Preheat the oven to 150°C/300°F/Gas 2.

3 Heat a hand-held waffle iron over the heat. Stir the batter and add more milk if required (the consistency should be quite thick). Open the waffle iron and pour some batter over two thirds of the surface. Close it and wipe off any excess batter.

4 Cook for 3–4 minutes, carefully turning the waffle iron over once during cooking. If using an electric waffle maker, follow the manufacturer's instructions for cooking.

5 When the batter stops steaming, open the iron and lift out the waffle with a fork. Put it on a heatproof plate and keep it hot in the oven. Repeat with the remaining batter to make eight waffles in all. Preheat the grill.

6 Cook the bananas: spread them out on a large shallow baking tin and top with the nuts. Scatter over the demerara sugar. Mix the maple syrup and rum together and spoon over.

7 Grill for 3–4 minutes or until the sugar begins to bubble. Serve on top of the waffles with single cream.

COOK'S TIP
If you don't own a waffle iron, prepare the batter as directed, but make small pancakes in a heavy-based frying pan. Alternatively, use ready-made waffles, which are available from large supermarkets, and reheat as directed on the packet before serving with the hot banana topping.

VARIATIONS
Use other fruits for the waffle topping, if you like. Small chunks of fresh or drained, canned pineapple, thin wedges of peaches or nectarines or even orange slices would be delicious alternatives to the banana.

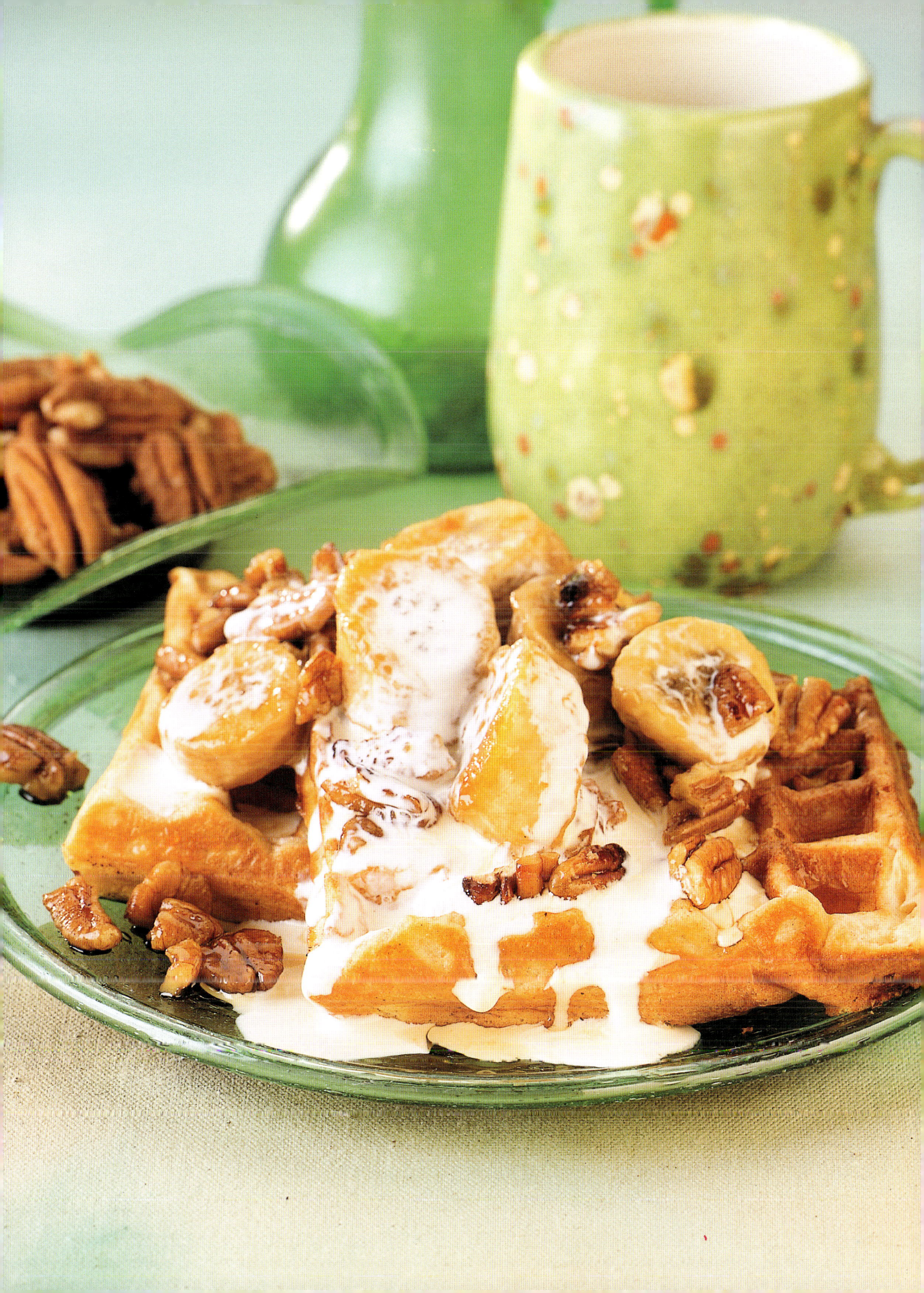

Mango and Tamarillo Pastries

These fruit-topped little pastries go down a treat with a cup of afternoon tea.

MAKES EIGHT

INGREDIENTS
225g/8oz ready-rolled puff pastry (30 × 25cm/12 × 10in rectangle)
1 egg yolk, lightly beaten
115g/4oz/½ cup white marzipan
40ml/8 tsp ginger or apricot conserve
1 mango, peeled and thinly sliced off the stone
2 tamarillos, halved and sliced
caster sugar, for sprinkling

1 Preheat the oven to 200°C/400°F/Gas 6. Unroll the pastry and cut it into 8 rectangles. Place on baking sheets.

VARIATION
Use apricot slices instead of tamarillos, or a mix of plums and peaches.

2 Using a sharp knife, score the surface of each piece of pastry into a diamond pattern, then brush with the egg yolk to glaze. Cut eight thin slices of marzipan and lay one slice on each pastry rectangle. Top each with a teaspoon of the ginger or apricot conserve and spread over evenly.

3 Top the pastry rectangles with alternate slices of mango and tamarillo. Sprinkle with some of the caster sugar, then bake for 15–20 minutes until the pastry is well puffed up and golden. Remove the pastries to a wire rack to cool. Sprinkle with more caster sugar before serving.

Exotic Fruit Tranche

This is a good way to make the most of a small selection of exotic fruit.

SERVES EIGHT

INGREDIENTS
- 175g/6oz/1½ cups plain flour
- 50g/2oz/¼ cup unsalted butter
- 25g/1oz/2 tbsp white vegetable fat
- 50g/2oz/¼ cup caster sugar
- 2 egg yolks
- about 15ml/1 tbsp cold water
- 115g/4oz/scant ½ cup apricot conserve, sieved and warmed

For the filling
- 150ml/¼ pint/⅔ cup double cream, plus extra to serve
- 250g/9oz/generous 1 cup mascarpone cheese
- 25g/1oz/¼ cup icing sugar, sifted
- grated rind of 1 orange
- 450g/1lb/3 cups mixed prepared fruits, such as mango, papaya, star fruit, kiwi fruit and blackberries
- 90ml/6 tbsp apricot conserve, sieved
- 15ml/1 tbsp white or coconut rum

1 Sift the flour into a bowl and rub in the butter and white vegetable fat until the mixture resembles fine breadcrumbs. Stir in the caster sugar. Add the egg yolks and enough cold water to make a soft dough. Thinly roll out the pastry between two sheets of clear film and use the pastry to line a 35 × 12cm/14 × 4½in fluted tranche tin. Allow the excess pastry to hang over the edge of the tin and chill for 30 minutes.

2 Preheat the oven to 200°C/400°F/Gas 6. Prick the base of the pastry case and line with non-stick baking paper and baking beans. Bake for 10–12 minutes. Lift out the paper and beans and return the pastry case to the oven for 5 minutes. Trim off the excess pastry and brush the inside of the case with the warmed apricot conserve to form a seal. Leave to cool on a wire rack.

3 Make the filling. Whip the cream to soft peaks, then stir it into the mascarpone with the icing sugar and orange rind. Spread in the cooled pastry case and top with the prepared fruits. Warm the apricot conserve with the rum and drizzle or brush over the fruits to make a glaze. Serve with extra cream.

COOK'S TIP
If you don't have a tranche tin, line a 23cm/9in flan tin with the pastry.

Banana and Pecan Bread

Bananas and pecans just seem to belong together. This is a really moist and delicious tea bread. Spread it with cream cheese or jam, or serve as a dessert with whipped cream.

MAKES A 900G/2LB LOAF

INGREDIENTS

115g/4oz/½ cup butter, softened
175g/6oz/1 cup light muscovado sugar
2 large eggs, beaten
3 ripe bananas
75g/3oz/¾ cup pecan nuts, coarsely chopped
225g/8oz/2 cups self-raising flour
2.5ml/½ tsp ground mixed spice

1 Preheat the oven to 180°C/350°F/Gas 4. Generously grease a 900g/2lb loaf tin and line it with non-stick baking paper. Cream the butter and muscovado sugar in a large mixing bowl until the mixture is light and fluffy. Gradually add the eggs, beating after each addition, until well combined.

2 Peel and then mash the bananas with a fork. Add them to the creamed mixture with the chopped pecan nuts. Beat until well combined.

COOK'S TIP
If the mixture shows signs of curdling when you add the eggs, stir in a little of the flour to stabilize it.

3 Sift the flour and mixed spice together and fold into the banana mixture. Spoon into the tin, level the surface and bake for 1–1¼ hours or until a skewer inserted into the middle of the loaf comes out clean. Cool for 10 minutes in the tin, then invert the tin on a wire rack. Lift off the tin, peel off the lining paper and cool completely.

Date and Walnut Brownies

These rich brownies are great for afternoon tea, but they also make a fantastic dessert. Reheat slices briefly in the microwave oven and serve with crème fraîche.

MAKES TWELVE

INGREDIENTS

350g/12oz plain chocolate, broken into squares
225g/8oz/1 cup butter, diced
3 large eggs
115g/4oz/½ cup caster sugar
5ml/1 tsp pure vanilla essence
75g/3oz/¾ cup plain flour, sifted
225g/8oz/1½ cups fresh dates, peeled, stoned and chopped
200g/7oz/1¾ cups walnut pieces
icing sugar, for dusting

COOK'S TIP
When melting the chocolate and butter, keep the water in the pan beneath hot, but do not let it approach boiling point. Chocolate is notoriously sensitive to heat; it is vital not to let it get too hot or it may stiffen into an unmanageable mass.

1 Preheat the oven to 190°C/375°F/Gas 5. Generously grease a 30 x 20cm/12 x 8in baking tin and line with non-stick baking paper.

2 Put the chocolate and butter in a large heatproof bowl. Place the bowl over a pan of hot water and leave until both have melted. Stir until smooth, then lift the bowl out and cool slightly.

3 In a separate bowl, beat the eggs, sugar and vanilla. Beat into the chocolate mixture, then fold in the flour, dates and nuts. Pour into the tin.

4 Bake for 30–40 minutes, until firm and the mixture comes away from the sides of the tin. Cool in the tin, then turn out, remove the paper and dust with icing sugar.

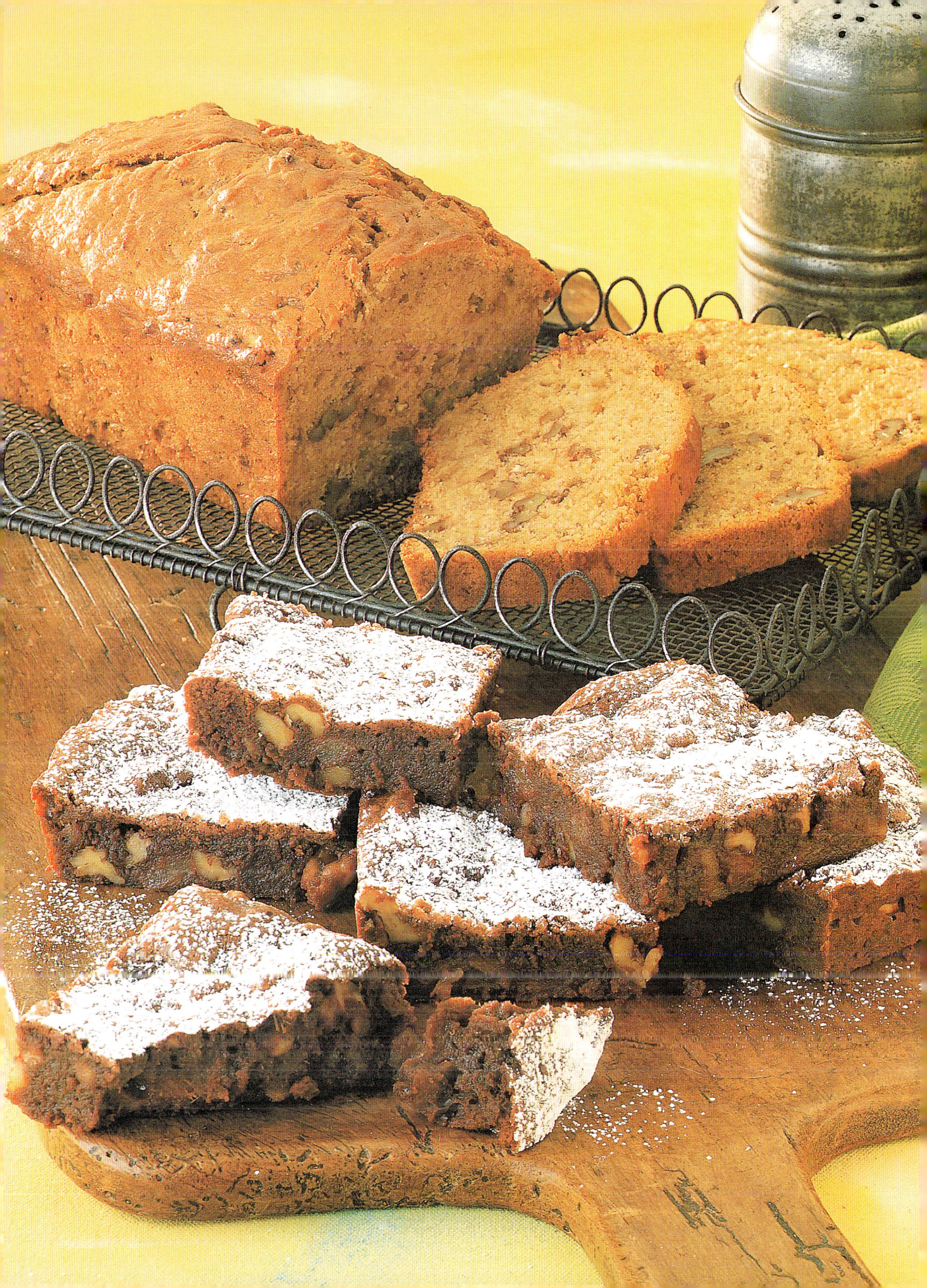

Mango Chutney

THIS CLASSIC CHUTNEY IS CONVENTIONALLY SERVED WITH CURRIES AND INDIAN POPPADOMS, BUT IT IS ALSO DELICIOUS WITH BAKED HAM OR A TRADITIONAL CHEESE PLOUGHMAN'S LUNCH.

MAKES 450G/1LB

INGREDIENTS

3 firm green mangoes
150ml/¼ pint/⅔ cup cider vinegar
130g/4½oz/⅔ cup light muscovado sugar
1 small red finger chilli or jalapeño chilli, split
2.5cm/1in piece of fresh root ginger, peeled and finely chopped
1 garlic clove, finely chopped
5 cardamom pods, bruised
2.5ml/½ tsp coriander seeds, crushed
1 bay leaf
2.5ml/½ tsp salt

1 Peel the mangoes and cut the flesh off the stone. Slice the mangoes lengthways, then cut across into small chunks or thin wedges.

2 Place these in a large saucepan, add the vinegar and cover. Cook over a low heat for 10 minutes.

3 Stir in the muscovado sugar, chilli, ginger, garlic, bruised cardamoms and coriander. Add the bay leaf and salt. Bring to the boil slowly, stirring often.

4 Lower the heat and simmer, uncovered, for 30 minutes or until the mixture is thick and syrupy.

5 Ladle into hot sterilized jars, seal and label. Store for 1 week before eating. Keep chilled after opening.

Papaya and Lemon Relish

This chunky relish is best made with a firm, unripe papaya. It should be left for a week before eating to allow all the flavours to mellow. Store the unopened jars in a cool place, away from sunlight. Serve with roast meats or with a robust cheese and crackers.

MAKES 450G/1LB

INGREDIENTS
- 1 large unripe papaya
- 1 onion, thinly sliced
- 40g/1½oz/⅓ cup raisins
- 250ml/8fl oz/1 cup red wine vinegar
- juice of 2 lemons
- 150ml/¼ pint/⅔ cup elderflower cordial
- 165g/5½oz/¾ cup golden granulated sugar
- 1 cinnamon stick
- 1 fresh bay leaf
- 2.5ml/½ tsp hot paprika
- 2.5ml/½ tsp salt

1 Peel the papaya and cut it lengthways in half. Remove the seeds with a small teaspoon. Cut the flesh into small chunks and place them in a large saucepan.

2 Add the onion slices and raisins to the papaya chunks, then stir in the vinegar. Bring to a boil, lower the heat and simmer for 10 minutes.

3 Add all the remaining ingredients and bring to the boil, stirring all the time. Check that all the sugar has dissolved, then lower the heat and simmer for 50–60 minutes or until the relish is thick and syrupy.

4 Ladle into hot sterilized jars. Seal and label and store for 1 week before using. Keep chilled after opening.

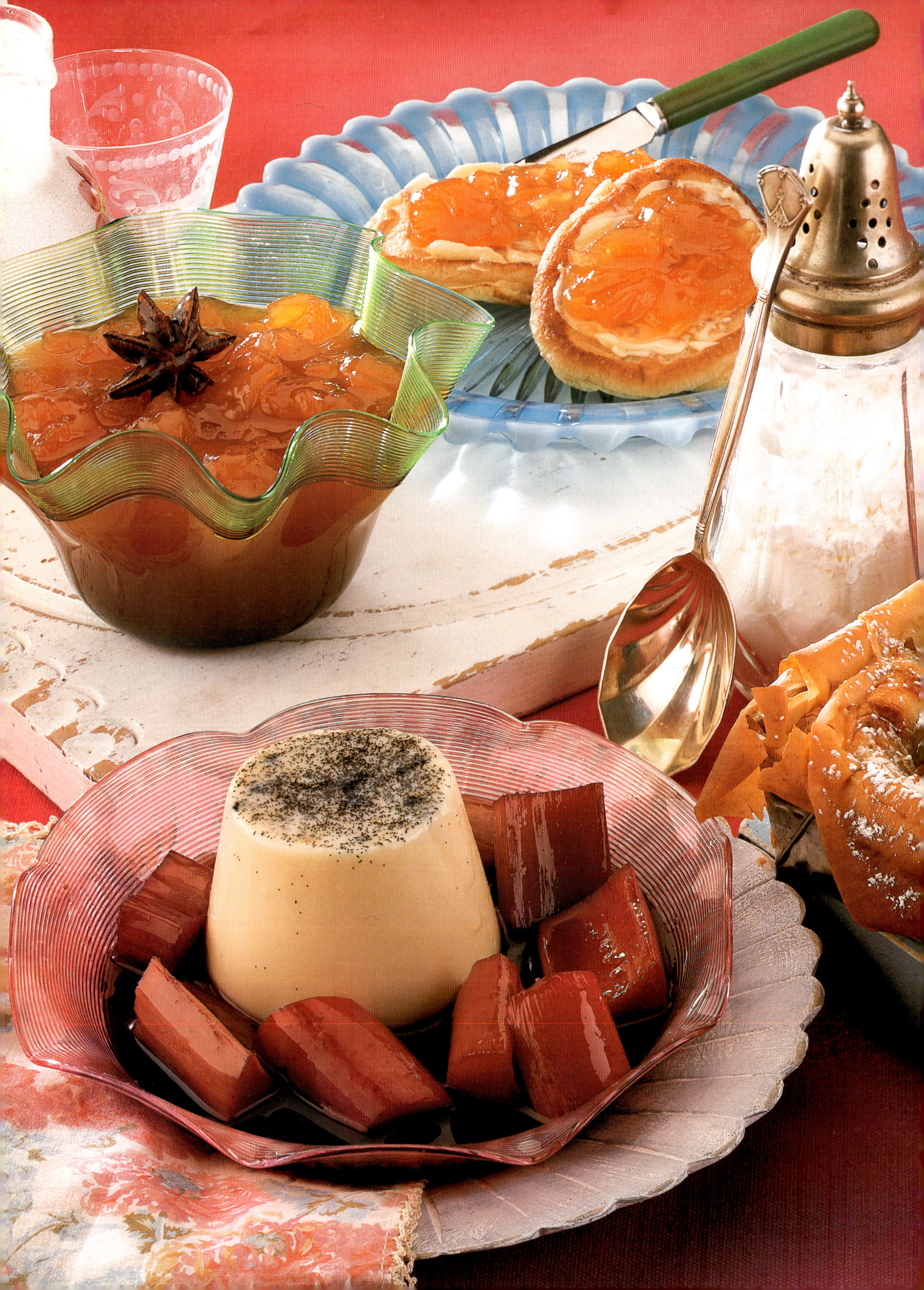

Melon, Grape, Fig and Rhubarb Recipes

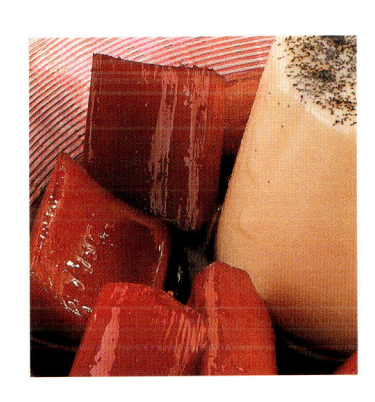

Whether alone or with other fruits, melons, rhubarb, figs and grapes make wonderful desserts, pies, cakes and preserves. Don't miss Red Grape and Cheese Tartlets, One-crust Rhubarb Pie or Greek Yogurt and Fig Cake.

MELON TRIO WITH GINGER BISCUITS

THE EYE-CATCHING COLOURS OF THESE THREE DIFFERENT MELONS REALLY MAKE THIS DESSERT, WHILE THE CRISP BISCUITS PROVIDE A PERFECT CONTRAST IN TERMS OF TEXTURE.

SERVES FOUR

INGREDIENTS
- ¼ watermelon
- ½ honeydew melon
- ½ charentais melon
- 60ml/4 tbsp stem ginger syrup

For the biscuits
- 25g/1oz/2 tbsp unsalted butter
- 25g/1oz/2 tbsp caster sugar
- 5ml/1 tsp clear honey
- 25g/1oz/¼ cup plain flour
- 25g/1oz/¼ cup luxury glacé mixed fruit, finely chopped
- 1 piece of stem ginger in syrup, drained and finely chopped
- 30ml/2 tbsp flaked almonds

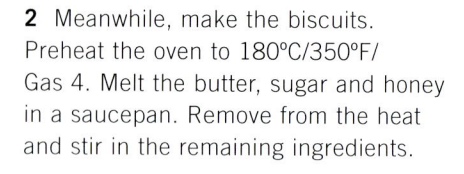

1 Remove the seeds from the melons, cut them into wedges, then slice off the rind. Cut all the flesh into chunks and mix in a bowl. Stir in the ginger syrup, cover and chill until ready to serve.

2 Meanwhile, make the biscuits. Preheat the oven to 180°C/350°F/Gas 4. Melt the butter, sugar and honey in a saucepan. Remove from the heat and stir in the remaining ingredients.

3 Line a baking sheet with non-stick baking paper. Space four spoonfuls of the mixture on the paper at regular intervals, leaving plenty of room for spreading. Flatten the mixture slightly into rounds and bake for 15 minutes or until the tops are golden.

4 Let the biscuits cool on the baking sheet for 1 minute, then lift each one in turn, using a fish slice, and drape over a rolling pin to cool and harden. Repeat with the remaining ginger mixture to make eight biscuits in all.

5 Serve the melon chunks with some of the syrup and the ginger biscuits.

COOK'S TIP
For an even prettier effect, scoop the melon flesh into balls with the large end of a melon baller.

Port-Stewed Rhubarb with Vanilla Desserts

RHUBARB IS ONE OF THOSE FRUITS THAT SELDOM REALIZES ITS FULL POTENTIAL. IT HAS QUITE A SHORT SEASON, SO IF YOU CAN REMEMBER IT IS WORTH FREEZING SOME FOR USE LATER IN THE YEAR.

SERVES FOUR

INGREDIENTS
- 115g/4oz/½ cup granulated sugar
- 150ml/¼ pint/⅔ cup water
- pared rind and juice of 1 orange
- 1 cinnamon stick
- 300ml/½ pint/1¼ cups ruby port
- 275g/10oz/2 cups rhubarb, cut into 2.5cm/1in pieces

For the vanilla desserts
- ¾ vanilla pod
- 175ml/6 fl oz/¾ cup double cream
- 175ml/6fl oz/¾ cup creamy milk
- 45ml/3 tbsp caster sugar
- 30ml/2 tbsp water
- 7.5ml/1½ tsp powdered gelatine

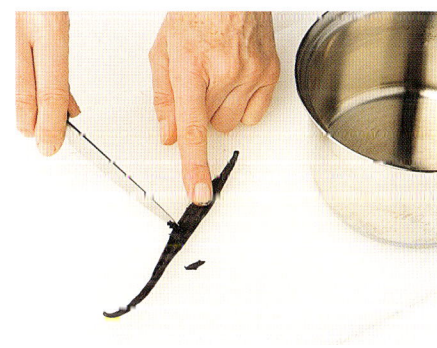

1 Start by making the vanilla desserts. Grease four individual pudding moulds or tins. Split the vanilla pod and scrape the seeds into a small saucepan. Add the pod, cream, milk and caster sugar. Simmer gently for 5 minutes, stirring.

2 Meanwhile, pour the water into a ramekin and sprinkle the gelatine over the surface. Set aside to sponge for 5 minutes. Place the ramekin in a pan of hot water and leave until the gelatine is dissolved, stirring occasionally.

3 Add the gelatine mixture to the hot milk mixture and stir until dissolved. Remove the vanilla pod and pour the mixture into the moulds or tins. Cool, then chill overnight or until set.

4 Put the sugar into a pan and add the water, orange rind and juice, and the cinnamon stick. Bring to the boil over a low heat, stirring occasionally until the sugar has dissolved. Increase the heat and boil for 1 minute.

5 Add the port, let the syrup return to the boil, then lower the heat and simmer for 15 minutes or until it has reduced and thickened. Remove the orange rind and cinnamon stick, add the rhubarb, cover and simmer gently for 2–3 minutes without stirring. Cool.

6 To serve, run a knife around the edge of each vanilla dessert to loosen it, then unmould on to a dessert plate. Serve each dessert with a spoonful or two of the rhubarb with its syrup.

COOK'S TIP
Rhubarb yields a lot of juice when cooked, so make sure the syrup has reduced well before adding the fruit.

Fig and Walnut Torte

This recipe is based on the traditional Middle Eastern speciality, baklava. It is sweet, sticky and delicious, and the figs add a refreshing touch. Since it is quite rich, plan on cutting the torte into fairly small diamonds – lovely with a cup of strong black coffee.

MAKES 20–25 PIECES

INGREDIENTS
- 75g/3oz/⅓ cup butter, melted, plus extra for greasing
- 175g/6oz/1½ cups walnuts, finely chopped
- 115g/4oz/1 cup ground almonds
- 75g/3oz/⅓ cup caster sugar
- 10ml/2 tsp ground cinnamon
- 9 large sheets of filo pastry, thawed if frozen, each cut into two 30 × 20cm/12 × 8in rectangles
- 4 fresh figs, sliced
- Greek yogurt, to serve

For the syrup
- 350g/12oz/1½ cups caster sugar
- 4 whole cloves
- 1 cinnamon stick
- 2 strips of lemon rind

1 Preheat the oven to 160°C/325°F/Gas 3. Generously grease a 30 × 20cm/12 × 8in shallow baking tin with melted butter. Mix together the walnuts, ground almonds, sugar and cinnamon in a bowl and set aside.

2 Fit a sheet of filo pastry in the base of the baking tin. Brush with some of the melted butter and place another sheet of filo on top. Repeat this until you have layered up eight sheets.

COOK'S TIP
Paper-thin filo pastry is delicate and dries out quickly. Work with one sheet at a time, and keep the other sheets covered or they will dry out.

3 Spoon half the nut mixture evenly over the filo pastry, right to the edges, and top with the fig slices.

4 Place two filo sheets on top of the figs, brushing each with more melted butter as before, then evenly spoon over the remaining nut mixture.

5 Layer the remaining filo sheets on top, buttering each one. Brush any remaining melted butter over the top of the torte, then score the surface with a sharp knife to give a diamond pattern. Bake for 1 hour until golden.

6 Meanwhile, make the syrup. Place all the ingredients in a saucepan and mix well. Heat, stirring, until the sugar has dissolved. Bring to the boil, lower the heat and simmer for 10 minutes until syrupy, stirring occasionally.

7 Allow the syrup to cool for about 15 minutes, then strain it evenly over the hot torte.

8 Allow to cool and soak for 2–3 hours, then cut the torte into diamonds or squares and serve with Greek yogurt. Store the torte in an airtight tin for up to three days.

VARIATION
If you like, replace the chopped walnuts with coarsely chopped pistachio nuts, or use finely chopped cashew nuts for an ultra-rich flavour.

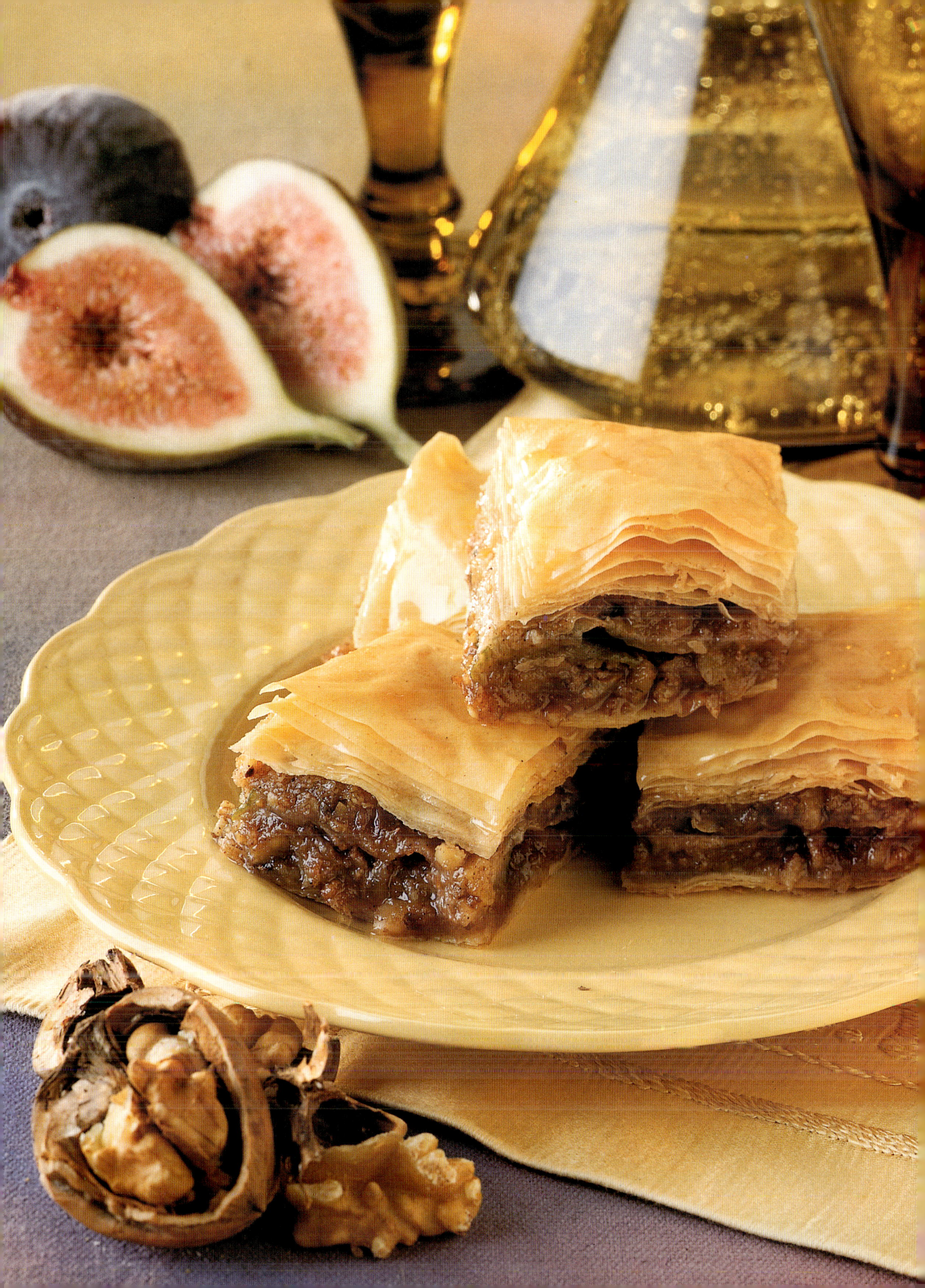

RED GRAPE AND CHEESE TARTLETS

FRUIT AND CHEESE IS A NATURAL COMBINATION IN THIS SIMPLE RECIPE. LOOK OUT FOR THE PALE, MAUVE-COLOURED OR RED GRAPES THAT TEND TO BE SLIGHTLY SMALLER THAN BLACK GRAPES. THESE ARE OFTEN SEEDLESS AND HAVE THE ADDED ADVANTAGE OF BEING SWEETER.

MAKES SIX

INGREDIENTS
350g/12oz sweet shortcrust pastry, thawed if frozen
225g/8oz/1 cup curd cheese
150ml/¼ pint/⅔ cup double cream
2.5ml/½ tsp pure vanilla essence
30ml/2 tbsp icing sugar
200g/7oz/2 cups red grapes, halved, seeded if necessary
60ml/4 tbsp apricot conserve
15ml/1 tbsp water

VARIATIONS
Use cranberry jelly or redcurrant jelly for the glaze. There will be no need to sieve either of these. Also vary the fruit topping, if you like. Try blackberries, blueberries, raspberries, sliced strawberries, kiwi fruit slices, banana slices or well-drained pineapple slices.

1 Preheat the oven to 200°C/400°F/Gas 6. Roll out the pastry and line six deep 9cm/3½in fluted individual tartlet tins. Prick the bases and line with non-stick baking paper and baking beans. Bake for 10 minutes, remove the paper and beans, then return the cases to the oven for 5 minutes until golden and fully cooked. Remove the pastry cases from the tins and cool on a wire rack.

2 Meanwhile, beat the curd cheese, double cream, vanilla essence and icing sugar in a bowl. Divide the mixture among the pastry cases. Smooth the surface and arrange the halved grapes on top.

3 Sieve the apricot conserve into a pan. Add the water and heat, stirring, until smooth. Spoon over the grapes. Cool, then chill before serving.

One-crust Rhubarb Pie

This method can be used for all sorts of fruit and is really foolproof. It doesn't matter how rough the pie looks when it goes into the oven; it comes out looking fantastic!

SERVES SIX

INGREDIENTS
350g/12oz shortcrust pastry, thawed if frozen
1 egg yolk, beaten
25g/1oz/3 tbsp semolina
25g/1oz/¼ cup hazelnuts, coarsely chopped
30ml/2 tbsp golden granulated sugar

For the filling
450g/1lb rhubarb, cut into 2.5cm/1in pieces
75g/3oz/⅓ cup caster sugar
1–2 pieces stem ginger in syrup, drained and finely chopped

COOK'S TIP
Egg yolk glaze brushed on to pastry gives it a nice golden sheen. However, be careful not to drip the glaze on the baking sheet, or it will burn and be difficult to remove.

1 Preheat the oven to 200°C/400°F/Gas 6. Roll out the pastry to a circle 35cm/14in across. Lay it over the rolling pin and transfer it to a large baking sheet. Brush a little egg yolk over the pastry. Scatter the semolina over the centre, leaving a wide rim all round.

2 Make the filling. Place the rhubarb pieces, caster sugar and chopped ginger in a large bowl and mix well.

3 Pile the rhubarb mixture into the middle of the pastry. Fold the rim roughly over the filling so that it almost covers it. Some of the fruit will remain visible in the centre.

4 Glaze the pastry rim with any remaining egg yolk and scatter the hazelnuts and golden sugar over. Bake for 30–35 minutes or until the pastry is golden brown. Serve warm.

Fresh Fig Filo Tart

Figs cook wonderfully well and taste superb in this tart — the riper the figs, the better.

SERVES SIX TO EIGHT

INGREDIENTS

five 35 × 25cm/14 × 10in sheets filo pastry, thawed if frozen
25g/1oz/2 tbsp butter, melted, plus extra for greasing
6 fresh figs, cut into wedges
75g/3oz/¾ cup plain flour
75g/3oz/⅓ cup caster sugar
4 eggs
450ml/¾ pint/1¾ cups creamy milk
2.5ml/½ tsp almond essence
15ml/1 tbsp icing sugar, for dusting
whipped cream or Greek yogurt, to serve

1 Preheat the oven to 190°C/375°F/Gas 5. Grease a 25 × 16cm/10 × 6¼in baking tin with butter. Brush each filo sheet in turn with melted butter and use to line the prepared tin.

2 Using scissors, cut off any excess pastry, leaving a little overhanging the edge. Arrange the figs in the filo case.

3 Sift the flour into a bowl and stir in the caster sugar. Add the eggs and a little of the milk and whisk until smooth. Gradually whisk in the remaining milk and the almond essence. Pour the mixture over the figs; bake for 1 hour or until the batter has set and is golden.

4 Remove the tart from the oven and allow it to cool in the tin on a wire rack for 10 minutes. Dust with the icing sugar and serve with whipped cream or Greek yogurt.

GREEK YOGURT AND FIG CAKE

BAKED FRESH FIGS, THICKLY SLICED, MAKE A DELECTABLE BASE FOR A FEATHERLIGHT SPONGE. FIGS THAT ARE A BIT ON THE FIRM SIDE WORK BEST FOR THIS PARTICULAR RECIPE.

SERVES SIX TO EIGHT

INGREDIENTS
- 6 firm fresh figs, thickly sliced
- 45ml/3 tbsp clear honey, plus extra for glazing cooked figs
- 200g/7oz/scant 1 cup butter, softened
- 175g/6oz/¾ cup caster sugar
- grated rind of 1 lemon
- grated rind of 1 orange
- 4 eggs, separated
- 225g/8oz/2 cups plain flour
- 5ml/1 tsp baking powder
- 5ml/1 tsp bicarbonate of soda
- 250ml/8fl oz/1 cup Greek yogurt

1 Preheat the oven to 180°C/350°F/Gas 4. Grease a 23cm/9in cake tin and line the base with non-stick baking paper. Arrange the figs over the base of the tin and drizzle over the honey.

2 In a large mixing bowl, cream the butter and caster sugar with the lemon and orange rinds until the mixture is pale and fluffy, then gradually beat in the egg yolks.

3 Sift the dry ingredients together. Add a little to the creamed mixture, beat well, then beat in a spoonful of Greek yogurt. Repeat this process until all the dry ingredients and Greek yogurt have been incorporated.

4 Whisk the egg whites in a grease-free bowl until they form stiff peaks. Stir half the whites into the cake mixture to slacken it slightly, then fold in the rest. Pour the mixture over the figs in the tin, then bake for 1¼ hours or until golden and a skewer inserted in the centre of the cake comes out clean.

5 Turn the cake out on to a wire rack, peel off the lining paper and cool. Drizzle the figs with extra honey before serving.

Melon and Star Anise Jam

Melon and ginger are classic companions. The addition of star anise imparts a wonderful oriental flavour to the jam. It's splendid on toasted fruit and spice muffins.

MAKES 450G/1LB

INGREDIENTS

2 charentais or cantaloupe melons, peeled and seeded
450g/1lb/2 cups granulated sugar
2 star anise
4 pieces stem ginger in syrup, drained and finely chopped
finely grated rind and juice of 2 lemons

COOK'S TIPS
Use this jam in savoury dishes instead of honey to add a spicy, non-cloying sweetness. Jams require a large amount of sugar for proper jelling – don't cut back.

1 Cut the melons into small cubes and layer with the granulated sugar in a large non-metallic bowl. Cover with clear film and leave overnight so the melons can release their juices.

2 Tip the melons and juice into a large saucepan and add the star anise, ginger, lemon rind and juice.

3 Bring to the boil, then lower the heat. Simmer for 25 minutes or until the melon has become transparent and the setting point has been reached. Test for this by spooning a small amount of the juice on to a chilled plate. If it wrinkles when you push a finger through the cooled liquid, it is ready to be potted.

4 Spoon the jam into hot sterilized jars. Seal, label and store in a cool, dry place. Once a jar has been opened, keep it in the fridge.

Fig and Date Chutney

This recipe is usually made with dried figs and dates, but it works perfectly well with fresh fruit and has a superb flavour. Try it with cream cheese on brown bread.

MAKES 450G/1LB

INGREDIENTS

- 1 orange
- 5 large fresh figs, coarsely chopped
- 350g/12oz/2½ cups fresh dates, peeled, stoned and chopped
- 2 onions, chopped
- 5cm/2in piece of fresh root ginger, peeled and finely grated
- 5ml/1 tsp dried crushed chillies
- 300g/11oz/1½ cups golden granulated sugar
- 300ml/½ pint/1¼ cups spiced preserving vinegar
- 2.5ml/½ tsp salt

1 Finely grate the rind of the orange, then cut off the remaining pith and segment the orange.

2 Place the orange segments in a large heavy-based saucepan with the chopped figs and dates. Add the rind, then stir in the onions, grated ginger, dried chillies, golden granulated sugar, spiced preserving vinegar and salt. Bring to the boil, stirring gently until all the sugar has dissolved.

3 Lower the heat and simmer gently for 1 hour or until the mixture has thickened and become pulpy, stirring often to prevent the mixture from sticking to the base of the pan.

4 Spoon the chutney into hot sterilized jars. Seal while still hot and label once the jars are cold. Store for 1 week before using. Once a jar has been opened, keep it in the fridge.

VARIATION

If you would rather use dried figs and dates to make the chutney, you will need to increase the amount of spiced preserving vinegar by 150ml/¼ pint/⅔ cup to 450ml/¾ pint/scant 2 cups. Stone the dates and coarsely chop the figs and dates.

Index

A

almonds
   cold lemon soufflé with caramelized almond topping, 77
   crunchy-topped fresh apricot cake, 41
   French apple tart, 21
   moist orange and almond cake, 84
   plum and marzipan pastries, 37
   yellow plum tart, 38

apples
   baked stuffed, 10
   and blackberry soufflés, 47
   charlottes, 15
   and cider sauce, 24
   crêpes, 12
   Dutch apple cake, 22
   filo-topped pie, 19
   French apple tart, 21
   recipes, 8–25
   and red onion marmalade, 24
   spiced apple crumble, 10
   tarte tatin, 18

apricots
   caramelized with pain perdu, 32
   crunchy-topped cake, 41
   exotic fruit tranche, 109
   parcels, 40

B

baked lattice peaches, 34

bananas
   with lime and cardamom sauce, 102
   and mascarpone creams, 102
   and pecan bread, 110
   and rum waffles, 106
   toffee bananas, 104

batter
   apple crêpes with butterscotch sauce, 12
   black cherry clafoutis, 30
   crêpes suzette, 74
   pear and cinnamon fritters, 13
   summer berry crêpes, 48

berries
   berry brûlée tarts, 62
   recipes, 44–65

black cherry clafoutis, 30

blackberries
   and apple soufflés, hot, 47
   bramble jelly, 64
   coconut jelly with star anise, 94
   exotic fruit tranche, 109
   spiced apple crumble, 10
   tropical fruit gratin, 98

blackcurrants
   berry brûlée tarts, 62
   bread and butter pudding, 58
   sorbet, 55
   summer pudding, 46

blueberries
   and cranberry streusel cake, 59
   fresh berry pavlova, 50
   fruits of the forest with white chocolate creams, 52
   muffins, 60
   pie, 61
   summer berry crêpes, 48
   summer pudding, 46

bramble jelly, 64
bread, banana and pecan, 110
bread and butter pudding, fresh currant, 58
brownies, date and walnut, 110
butterscotch sauce, apple crêpes with, 12

C

cakes
   cranberry and blueberry streusel, 59
   crunchy-topped fresh apricot, 41
   Dutch apple, 22
   Greek yogurt and fig, 123
   lemon and lime syrup, 85
   moist orange and almond, 84
   pear and polenta, 22

caramel
   baked lattice pears, 34
   caramelized apricots with pain perdu, 32
   crème caramels with dipped physalis, 91

charlottes, apple, 15

cheesecakes
   lemon and lime, 73
   pomegranate jewelled, 101

cherries
   black cherry clafoutis, 30
   and hazelnut strudel, 33

chocolate
   and mandarin truffle slice, 72
   pear and pecan pie, 20
   white chocolate creams, 52

chutneys
   fig and date, 125
   mango, 112
   pickled peach and chilli, 42

cider, and apple sauce, 24
cinnamon, and pear fritters, 13

citrus fruits
   citrus fruit flambé with pistachio praline, 76
   recipes, 66–87

clafoutis, black cherry, 30
clementine jelly, 69

coconut
   cold mango soufflés, 90
   jelly with star anise, 94

cointreau oranges, 68
cranberry and blueberry streusel cake, 59
crème caramels, passion fruit, 91

crêpes
   apple, 12
   summer berry, 48
   suzette, 74

crumble, spiced apple, 10
crunchy-topped fresh apricot cake, 41

currants (fresh)
   recipes, 44–65
   bread and butter pudding, 58

D

damson and gin soufflés, iced, 31

dates
   and fig chutney, 125
   hot puddings with toffee sauce, 105
   pickled peach and chilli chutney, 42
   and walnut brownies, 110

Dutch apple cake, 22

E

elderflowers
   and gooseberry fool, 51
   and lychee sorbet, 92

exotic fruits
   recipes, 88–113
   salad, 97
   sushi, 93
   tranche, 109

F

figs
   and date chutney, 125
   exotic fruit sushi, 93
   fresh fig filo tart, 122
   Greek yogurt and fig cake, 123
   and walnut torte, 118

filo pastry
   apple pie, 19
   fresh fig tart, 122

flambé, citrus fruit, with pistachio praline, 76
fool, gooseberry and elderflower, 51
French apple tart, 21
fritters, pear and cinnamon, 13
fruits of the forest with white chocolate creams, 52

G
gin and damson soufflés, 31
ginger
    baskets, ruby orange sherbet in, 70
    biscuits, with melon trio, 116
    papaya baked with, 96
gooseberry and elderflower fool, 51
grapefruit
    citrus fruit flambé, 76
    three-fruit marmalade, 86
grapes
    red grape and cheese tartlets, 120
gratin, tropical fruit, 98
Greek yogurt and fig cake, 123
greengages
    yellow plum tart, 38

H
hazelnuts
    and fresh cherry strudel, 33
    and nectarine meringues, 28

I
ice cream, fresh strawberry, 54
iced gin and damson soufflés, 31

J
Jamaican fruit trifle, 100
jams
    melon and star anise, 124
    strawberry, 65
    see also jellies

jellies
    bramble, 64
    clementine, 69
    coconut, with star anise fruits, 94

K
Key lime pie, 82
kiwi fruit
    exotic fruit salad, 97
    exotic fruit sushi, 93
    exotic fruit tranche, 109
kumquats, spiced poached, 86

L
lemon grass skewers with lime cheese, 94
lemons
    coeur à la crème with cointreau oranges, 68
    cold lemon soufflé with caramelized almond topping, 77
    crêpes suzette, 74
    fresh lemon tart, 81
    lemon curd cream, 78
    and lime cheesecake, 73
    and lime syrup cake, 85
    meringue pie, 80
    and papaya relish, 113
    roulade, 78
    surprise pudding, 74
limes
    and cardamom sauce, 102
    cheese, 94
    citrus fruit flambé, 76
    Key lime pie, 82
    and lemon cheesecake, 73
    and lemon syrup cake, 85
lychees
    coconut jelly with star anise fruits, 94
    and elderflower sorbet, 92

M
mandarins, and chocolate truffle slice, 72
mangoes
    chutney, 112
    cold mango soufflés topped with toasted coconut, 90
    exotic fruit salad, 97
    exotic fruit sushi, 93
    exotic fruit tranche, 109
    Jamaican fruit trifle, 100
    lemon grass skewers with lime cheese, 94
    and tamarillo pastries, 108
    tropical fruit gratin, 98
marmalades
    apple and red onion, 24
    three-fruit, 86
marzipan
    baked lattice peaches, 34
    and plum pastries, 37
mascarpone, and banana creams, 102
melons
    and star anise jam, 124
    trio with ginger biscuits, 116
meringues
    lemon meringue pie, 80
    nectarine and hazelnut, 28
mincemeat
    apricot parcels, 40
moist orange and almond cake, 84
muffins, fresh blueberry, 60

N
nectarines
    and hazelnut meringues, 28
    relish, 42

O
one-crust rhubarb pie, 121
onions
    apple and red onion marmalade, 24
oranges
    citrus fruit flambé, 76
    crêpes suzette, 74
    moist orange and almond cake, 84
    ruby orange sherbet in ginger baskets, 70
    three-fruit marmalade, 86

P
pain perdu, caramelized apricots with, 32
papayas
    baked with ginger, 96
    exotic fruit salad, 97
    exotic fruit tranche, 109
    lemon grass skewers with lime cheese, 94
    and lemon relish, 113
    sauce, 98
passion fruit
    crème caramels with dipped physalis, 91
    exotic fruit salad with, 97
pastry
    apricot parcels, 40
    baked lattice peaches, 34
    berry brûlée tarts, 62
    chocolate, pear and pecan pie, 20
    exotic fruit tranche, 109
    filo-topped apple pie, 19
    French apple tart, 21
    fresh cherry and hazelnut strudel, 33
    fresh fig and filo tart, 122
    fresh lemon tart, 81
    key lime pie, 82
    lemon meringue pie, 80
    mango and tamarillo pastries, 108
    one-crust rhubarb pie, 121
    peach and redcurrant tartlets, 36
    plum and marzipan pastries, 37
    red grape and cheese tartlets, 120
    tarte tatin, 18
    yellow plum tart, 38
pavlova, fresh berry, 50
peaches
    baked lattice peaches, 34

Index

peach melba syllabub, 28
pickled peach and chilli
   chutney, 42
and redcurrant tartlets, 36
pears
   chocolate, pear and
      pecan pie, 20
   and cinnamon fritters, 13
   poached in port
      syrup, 14
   and polenta cake, 22
pecans
   baked stuffed apples, 10
   and banana bread, 110
   and chocolate and pear
      pie, 20
physalis, passion fruit crème
   caramels with, 91
pies
   blueberry, 61
   chocolate, pear and
      pecan, 20
   filo-topped apple, 19
   Key lime, 82
   lemon meringue, 80
   one-crust rhubarb, 121
pineapples
   grilled with papaya
      sauce, 98
   Jamaican fruit trifle, 100
   tropical fruit gratin, 98

plums
   and marzipan pastries, 37
   yellow plum tart, 38
polenta, and pear cake, 22
pomegranate jewelled
   cheesecake, 101
port-stewed rhubarb with
   vanilla desserts, 117
port syrup, pears in, 14
praline
   port flambé with pistachio
      praline, 76
preserves
   apple and red onion
      marmalade, 24
   bramble jelly, 64

fig and date chutney, 125
mango chutney, 112
melon and star anise
   jam, 124
nectarine relish, 42
papaya and lemon
   relish, 113
pickled peach and chilli
   chutney, 42
strawberry jam, 65
three-fruit marmalade, 86

Q
quince soufflés, hot, 16

R
raspberries
   fruits of the forest with
      white chocolate
      creams, 52
   peach melba syllabub, 28
   and rose petal
      shortcakes, 56
   summer berry crêpes, 48
   summer pudding, 46
red grape and cheese
   tartlets, 120
redcurrants
   berry brûlée tarts, 62
   bread and butter
      pudding, 58
   and peach tartlets, 36
   summer berry crêpes, 48
   summer pudding, 46
relishes
   nectarine, 42
   papaya and lemon, 113
rhubarb
   one-crust pie, 121
   port-stewed, with vanilla
      desserts, 117
roulade, lemon, 78
ruby orange sherbet in
   ginger baskets, 70
rum and banana
   waffles, 106

S
sauces
   apple and cider, 24
   butterscotch, 12
   lime and cardamom, 102

toffee, 105
sherbet, ruby orange, in
   ginger baskets, 70
shortcakes, raspberry and
   rose petal, 56
sorbets
   blackcurrant, 55
   lychee and
      elderflower, 92
soufflés
   cold lemon, with
      caramelized almond
      topping, 77
   cold mango, topped with
      toasted coconut, 90
   hot blackberry and
      apple, 47
   hot quince, 16
   iced gin and
      damson, 31
spiced apple crumble, 10
spiced poached
   kumquats, 86
star anise
   coconut jelly with, 94
   and melon jam, 124
star fruit
   coconut jelly with star
      anise fruits, 94
   exotic fruit sushi, 93
   exotic fruit tranche, 109
   lemon grass skewers with
      lime cheese, 94
stone fruit
   recipes, 26–43
strawberries
   berry brûlée tarts, 62
   ice cream, 54
   jam, 65
   summer berry
      crêpes, 48
   summer pudding, 46
streusel cake, 59
strudel, fresh cherry and
   hazelnut, 33
summer berry crêpes, 48
summer pudding, 46
sushi, exotic fruit, 93
syllabub, peach melba, 28
syrup, port, 14

T
tamarillos
   and mango pastries, 108
   tropical fruit gratin, 98
tarte tatin, 18

tarts
   berry brûlée, 62
   exotic fruit tranche, 109
   fig and walnut, 118
   French apple, 21
   fresh fig filo, 122
   fresh lemon, 81
   peach and redcurrant
      tartlets, 36
   red grape and cheese
      tartlets, 120
   tarte tatin, 18
   yellow plum, 38
three-fruit marmalade, 86
toffee bananas, 104
toffee sauce, hot date
   puddings with, 105
trifle, Jamaican fruit, 100
tropical fruit gratin, 98
truffle slice, chocolate and
   mandarin, 72

V
vanilla desserts, 117

W
waffles, rum and
   banana, 106
walnuts
   and date brownies, 110
   and fig torte, 118
watermelons
   melon trio with ginger
      biscuits, 116

Y
yellow plum tart, 38
yogurt and fig cake, 123